TRUE LOVE —IT'S IN THE NUMBERS!

Think of the hundreds and thousands of numbers that surround us every day—each and every one with a special meaning, a unique aura that colours our dreams and desires. Numerology has long provided great insight into the power of numbers. And just as the greatest pharaohs of Egypt and the most powerful emperors of Rome called upon this ancient science for direction, so can you, too, turn to the numbers for success in love today—and for many tomorrows to come.

IT ALL ADDS UP TO LOVE is the definitive guide to numerology. Providing the means to recognize and evaluate your most vital numbers—those in your name and birthdate, and in the most important days or months or years in your life—this insightful book will enable you to tap their numerological energy to the fullest. So look to the pages ahead to stack the romantic odds—and evens—in your favour and make the numbers work for you!

HELEN TONO, author of numerous books and articles on numerology, astrology, and the occult, makes her significant expertise available to both the experienced and beginning fan of numerology.

The Love Life Guides

Starring Your Love Life
It All Adds Up to Love
The Lover's Dream
Tarot: Love is in the Cards

IT ALL ADDS UP TO LOVE

Helen Tono

BANTAM BOOKS
TORONTO • NEW YORK • LONDON • SYDNEY • AUCKLAND

IT ALL ADDS UP TO LOVE

A BANTAM BOOK 0 553 40027 4

First publication in Great Britain

PRINTING HISTORY
Bantam Books edition published 1989

Bantam Books are published by Transworld Publishers Ltd., 61–63 Uxbridge Road, Ealing, London W5 5SA, in Australia by Transworld Publishers (Australia) Pty. Ltd., 15–23 Helles Avenue, Moorebank, NSW 2170, and in New Zealand by Transworld Publishers (N.Z.) Ltd., Cnr. Moselle and Waipareira Avenues, Henderson, Auckland.

Printed and bound in Great Britain by
Cox & Wyman Ltd., Reading, Berks.

IT ALL ADDS UP TO LOVE

IT ALL ADDS UP TO LOVE

CHAPTER I

Finding Your Numerical Vibrations

DID YOU EVER NOTICE THAT SOME DAYS seem almost magically good and everything goes better than even the best you could have imagined, while on other days absolutely nothing seems to go right? That at certain times love flows freely to and from you and you're deliriously happy, while during other periods Saturday nights become a lonely ritual of TV-watching? You may feel that this sense of harmony or discord was hit or miss—that some days you accidentally found it or it found you.

In reality, much of this fluctuation is due to changing numerical vibrations. Think of the hundreds—even thousands—of numbers that surround you each day. Every one of them has a numerical vibration that may affect your life (although some will have more of an impact than others)! You, too, have your own numerical vibrations, and depending upon whether your numbers are harmonious with the numbers associated with any given day or event or other person, you will have an easier or more difficult time with that day or event or person.

Knowing how to recognize and make the most of the numbers in your life—and your love—you'll be able to prepare and adjust your actions accordingly, to achieve great happiness and fulfillment. By attuning yourself to your personal numbers and to the universal vibrations around you, you'll be able to do the right thing at the right time, and find the right person for you!

Through an understanding of numerology, you can come to better know yourself: your strengths and weaknesses, your needs and desires—both those you openly acknowledge and those you hide away in your subconscious mind. Numerology will also help you understand other people—your wife or husband, lover, parents, boss, or friends. Whether your goal is to find and attract the right mate, to build lasting happiness with your present partner, or merely to enhance a friendship, numerology will provide you with the understanding and insight to stack the numbers in your favor!

The first step in using numerology is to find the numerical value of whatever you are interested in. You'll learn all the major things that have a numerological impact on your life in Chapter II, but to begin with, let's simply take your name. First of all, you must assign to each letter in your name its numerical value, and then you add up those values. The numerical values of the letters are as follows:

A	B	C	D	E	F	G	H	I	J	K	L	M	N	O	P
1	2	3	4	5	6	7	8	9	1	2	3	4	5	6	7

Q	R	S	T	U	V	W	X	Y	Z
8	9	1	2	3	4	5	6	7	8

You'll notice that only the numbers 1 through 9 are used. Numerology is based on single-digit numbers (except for the "master numbers," 11 and 22, which are discussed in greater detail in Chapter XIII; in everyday life and love, however, and for the purposes of this book, these master numbers equate to 2, or 1 + 1, for 11, and 4, or 2 + 2, for 22). Obviously, the letters in almost any name will add up to more than 9. The final single digit is arrived at by adding the final numbers. If the letters in your name total 34, for instance, your significant number is 7 (3 + 4). If your letters total 168, your final number is 6 (1 + 6 + 8 = 15 = 1 + 5 = 6). Zeros do not count and are dropped (i.e. 30 becomes 3, 105 becomes 15 which becomes 1 + 5, or 6). To illustrate how these numerical values are arrived at, let's take the name KAREN SUE ANDERSON:

K	A	R	E	N		S	U	E		A	N	D	E	R	S	O	N
2	1	9	5	5		1	3	5		1	5	4	5	9	1	6	5

Thus, 2 + 1 + 9, etc., equals 67, which then becomes 6 + 7 = 13 = 1 + 3, for a final total of 4.

Let's take another example:

J	O	H	N		A	M	E	S	
1	6	8	5		1	4	5	1	= 31 = 3 + 1 = 4.

As you have probably noticed, one of these names was quite long, the other unusually short, but exactly the same system was used to determine their numerical value. This is the only system used in numerology, regardless of whether you are figuring out a name, date, place, or anything else.

There is one very important thing to remember with regard to names, though: A person's basic nature is revealed by his or her name *exactly as it appears on the birth certificate*. Foreign spellings, mistakes in spelling, or any other deviation from the name as you know it, are not corrected for numerological purposes. If your name is Greene, for instance, and it appears on your birth certificate as Green, or if it is Crayne and it appears as Crain, Green and Crain are the names to use. Even if the birth certificate name is bizarre—if the parents hadn't yet decided on a name and the entry reads Baby Girl Smith, for instance, or if an unidentified infant is called John Doe—that's the name that indicates his or her basic character.

Of course, Baby Girl Smith eventually gets a name and becomes Jennifer Smith, and John Doe is adopted and becomes Jose Ramirez. Birth certificate names change for a variety of reasons, either by choice or through changing circumstances. Actors, rock musicians, and other performers often change their names to make them more appropriate to the personas they're trying to project to their audience. Even on a less public level, a bank president may think J. Carlton Smith sounds more impressive than John C. Smith. And a woman, when she marries, is often happy to trade her name for her husband's.

Numerologically, this name change indicates that the person involved has taken on an overlay, as it were, which doesn't change his or her basic nature but might change the circumstances of his or her life and the impression he or she makes on others. (The numerical value of the new name is, of course, arrived at by the same method used to find the value of the original name.) It is interesting to compare the two names and see what qualities are emphasized or pushed into the background by the change.

In addition to your name, another particularly important element in numerology is your birth date. This number is arrived at very simply, since a date is already composed mainly of numbers. The month is reduced to a number by calling January "1", February "2," and so on—just the way you write the month when abbreviating. Thus, June 12, 1957 becomes 6 + 1 + 2 + 1 + 9 + 5 + 7 = 31 = 3 + 1 = 4. Similarly, February 5, 1933, becomes 2 + 5 + 1 + 9 + 3 + 3 = 23 = 2 + 3 = 5. September 29, 1968 becomes 9 + 2 + 9 + 1 + 9 + 6 + 8 = 44 = 4 + 4 = 8. And so it goes. Any birth date is easily converted into a single digit.

Later chapters will describe the significance of numbers in various positions in the numerology chart. Here it might just be said that while name numbers describe an individual's personality, birth-date numbers describe the life experiences that individual is likely to have.

Naturally, apart from your name and birth date

many other numbers may be of great importance to you. Choosing a wedding date immediately comes to mind, but you might also be concerned about which day would be most fortuitous for starting your own business or initiating some major venture. You might even want to know the best day to plan a party or go on a trip. Similarly, you may want to look back to the past and see what influences were operating at the time of a major event in your life. The day you met your husband or wife, for example, the day you decided you wanted to get married, or alas, the day you may have chosen to call a relationship quits, chances are the numerical energy of that time played an important role in the event.

Any date—past, present, or future—can be easily calculated using the method described above. The result can then be compared to your name numbers to see how a particular date relates to you personally. And an address, a company name, the name of a college, hospital, or any other institution, or the name of any person, place, or thing, in fact, can be calculated and compared to your own numbers to see how it affects you. Remember, though, that each person's numerology chart has several important numbers, not just one. So, when making comparisons between that individual's chart and any other person, place, or thing, remember that some indicators can be favorable, others unfavorable.

But when you think about it, that's the way life is. Thus, numerology does not promise to find you the perfect mate, with whom you can live happily ever after. What it *does* help you do is to appraise realistically both yourself and your lover or prospective partner, so you can see where there are harmonies, and where there are differences. Then you can make wise decisions about what you can and cannot tolerate, which potentialities should be pursued in yourself and in your lover. In order to be truly happy in love it is necessary to understand yourself and your own priorities, desires, and goals. Numerology can help you attain this self-knowledge. Knowing the numbers are behind you, with the valuable insights they afford, and working hard to understand and wield their power, you can find romantic satisfaction and personal fulfillment in any number of different people and situations. Mr. or Ms. Right can take on many different faces; true love can be found in the oddest corners, colors, and shapes. And before long, you'll realize that the equation for love is not just in one number, but all around you!

CHAPTER II

YOUR PERSONAL NUMBERS

IF MORE PEOPLE WERE KNOWLEDGEABLE about numerology, they would not ask each other, "What's your sign?" upon meeting, but rather, "What's your number?" For just as your astrological sign characterizes your basic essence, so does numerology give great insight into your personality and potential. Unlike astrology, however, which places a primary importance on a single sign, your sun sign, numerology indicates no *one single* number which sums up your character. Relying on *several different* numbers—each of which indicates a different side of you and your potential—numerology takes a rather different, and in many ways more practical, approach to understanding our very complex natures.

Thus, the numerology "chart," as it is referred to throughout this book, is not based on any one particular number but on the play between a variety of different numbers, each of which shows a unique and separate insight into your character and potential in life. This chart does not take any concrete form (such as a vertical or horizontal column, etc.), but rather refers to the combined interplay of all the numerical influences described below.

Perhaps the most important number in the numerology chart is the Soul Urge, which is found by totaling the vowels (A, E, I, O, and U) in a person's name. Rather than describe the kind of person an individual is, this number indicates what he *wants to be*, what he strives for, what he hopes to achieve and in what way. In a sense, the Soul Urge is an individual's ideal vision of himself, somewhat like a role model which the individual tries to follow—both its noble and not so noble traits. While the word "soul" suggests spiritual connotations, here morality has nothing to do with it. Each person can make the choice for himself of using his traits constructively and positively, or negatively and destructively.

Not surprisingly, the Soul Urge is of vital importance in love, and must be considered when trying to find—and maintain—a happy, long-lasting relationship. If you are ambitious, for instance, a real go-getter who hopes to achieve great things in the world, and you meet someone who's fascinating and attractive, but whose Soul Urge indicates a desire for a quiet, family-oriented life, there will probably be rough times ahead for the two of you—if indeed you make it past the first date! Or if you are expansive, artistic, and free spending, you could be a constant source of irritation to a more stolid, thrifty type.

So check the Soul Urge of your next date and

see how it compares with your own. Since each of us invests a lot of energy striving to realize our Soul Urge—whether or not we know it—its general nature is usually very recognizable. If you are perceived as being the ambitious go-getter mentioned above, for example, your Soul Urge number will probably reflect that image. This is different from some of the other numbers, which represent more subtle or secret parts of ourselves and are slightly harder to gauge at first glance. Your Soul Urge is not a matter of intellect but of deep, often subconscious, instinct. Thus a relationship between two people with compatible Soul Urges has a lot going for it, because the energy associated with it is strong and not easily swayed by the other numbers in the numerology chart (although those numbers will, of course, add unique color and exert a certain influence).

Your Soul Urge is derived from just the vowels in your name, using the same number-for-letter values given in Chapter 1. For example, Olympic gymnast Mary Lou Retton's Soul Urge is, not surprisingly, the bold, ambitious, independent number 1 (since all zeros are automatically dropped in numerology):

```
MARY LOU RETTON
 1 7  6 3  5  6  = 28 =
2 + 8 = 10 = 1
```

You will note that in this case the consonant Y is included with the vowels. This is true *only* when a syllable has no vowel (that is, no A, E, I, O, or U); this usually occurs at the end of a word, as in Mary, Hen-ry, or Cath-y, although it also applies to names such as Bryce or Gwyn.

Let's try a few more examples to reinforce your understanding of how the Soul Urge is derived from the name:

```
HERMAN TAYLOR COLLINS
  5   1   1  6   6  9
= 28 = 10 = 1
```

Though a completely different name from Mary Lou Retton, this name also adds up to 1. (Note that the Y in Taylor is not counted as a vowel because there is a true vowel—A—in the same syllable.)

Now for one last example:

```
J O A N   C H U
  6 1         3  =  10  =  1
```

Here again, we end up with a Soul Urge of 1. These three names, each adding up to the same Soul Urge, were chosen not only as examples of how to find the Soul Urge number but also to illustrate another point: Though the final total is 1 in all three names, it is composed of different elements in each. Mary Lou Retton's name is Mary (8) Lou (9) Retton (11). (With the master number 11 in her last name, Mary Lou Retton will have some of the special qualities associated with that number, described in Chapter XIII, but for the purposes of this book this number is treated as 2.) Herman Taylor Collins's name is composed of Herman (6) Taylor (7) and Collins (6). Finally, Joan Chu's Soul Urge is composed of a 7 and a 3. This shows us that while all three of these people have the leadership qualities of the number 1, each will lead and accomplish in different ways, which will be influenced by the numerical Soul Urge value associated with their first, middle, and last names.

These differences are something to be considered when assessing the compatibility between two numerology charts. However, if both individuals have a Soul Urge of 1, they are at least both strivers and would-be achievers, regardless of the specific components adding up to that number. They will understand this quality in each other and will in all likelihood be supportive of each other's efforts. This is bound to create a certain respect between them, which is, of course, a big plus when it comes to love.

The second important number in your name is that of the Latent or Quiescent Self, which is composed of all the consonants (that is, everything *except* A, E, I, O, and U). This number is not active in itself, but represents you at rest. It expresses your private dreams and desires, which may or may not be quite different from those of your Soul Urge. In a sense, the Latent number is the true you; on the other hand, being quiescent, this number cannot be expressed in action and even *you* may not be fully aware of your innermost wishes. The nature of this number is much less obvious than that of your Soul Urge, which you work actively to attain.

Take the following example:

J E N N I F E R C A R O L R A Y M O N D
1 5 5 6 9 3 9 3 9 7 4 5 4
= 70 = 7

As with the Soul Urge, this number can be broken down into its components to add detail to the portrait the numerology chart is painting: Jennifer (8) Carol (6) Raymond (11). Again, though, when assessing the Latent number of any potential Mr. or Ms. Right, if their final total is the same as yours, this is a plus! The two of you are bound to have a certain basic similarity in your *inner* desires, even if you differ in minor ways or in the goals you *outwardly* pursue.

The third important number associated with your name is your Expression, which is the total value of all the letters in your name, both vowels and consonants. To put it in words rather than numbers, the Expression is the manner in which both your Latent self (who you are) and your Soul Urge (what you want to be or do) manifest themselves in action—or express themselves, so to speak. Though, of course, there are infinite variations in the details. People with the same Soul Urge number and Latent number combining to form an identical Expression number express themselves in certain generally similar ways. Of course, as with the Soul Urge, each Expression number can also be broken down into its components, which again makes for variation. For example, an 8 Expression may be made up of 1 + 7, 2 + 6, 3 + 5, 4 + 4, 5 + 3, 6 + 2, or 7 + 1. (There's a big difference between a Soul Urge and a Latent number of 1, as you can see from preceding descriptions.)

Since the Expression is the sum of the vowels (Soul Urge) and consonants (Latent number), you can find it by simply adding up these two figures. Taking our previous example, we can calculate the Expression as follows:

```
 5  9 5    1 6    1   6
JENNIFER CAROL RAYMOND  = 33 = 6
1 55 6 93  9  39  74  54 = 70 = 7
```

Vowels are usually placed above the name and are counted first, to arrive at the Soul Urge. Consonants are placed below the name and are counted next, to arrive at the Latent number. Then the top and bottom figures are both counted as if they were one continuous column.

Thus, in the case of Jennifer Carol Raymond, we add 1 + 5 + 5 + 5 +9 + 6 + 5 + 9 + 3 + 1 + 9 + 6 + 3 + 9 + 1 + 7 + 4 + 6 + 5 + 4. (There's nothing wrong with using a pocket calculator if you have one!) And the result is 103, or 1 + 3 = 4. This, not coincidentally, is exactly the same as the sum of 6 (Soul Urge) + 7 (Latent number) = 13 = 1 + 3 = 4. So with this double check you know your figures are correct.

Using these three numbers you can arrive at the basics of an individual's personality. But in addition to the Soul Urge, Latent number, and Expression, there are two more numbers that are also important in numerology: One is your birth date, which shows your Life Path, and the other is the combination of your Expression number and your birth date, which is called your Life Purpose. As explained in Chapter I, the birth date number is derived from the birth month (expressed in figures from 1 through 12) plus the day and year, which are already figures.

The Life Path indicates the type of experiences a person is likely to have during his or her lifetime. Of course, this is very general, since all of an individual's experiences couldn't possibly be compressed into a single number. Yet the person whose Life Path number is 1 will have more opportunities for leadership than will receptive 2 or artistic 3, for example. And other factors in the numerology chart will add detail—notably the individual's personality, as expressed by his or her Soul Urge, Latent, and Expression numbers. You may be on a Life Path that is relatively easy for you or one which is difficult and challenging. After all, not everyone who has opportunities for leadership is a natural leader; he may have chances and fail. Similarly, someone with great leadership potential may find himself, through the unpredictable force of circumstance, lacking opportunities to express his possibilities.

The Life Purpose expresses what you are expected to achieve in life. This number carries certain spiritual connotations. Many numerologists ignore the Life Purpose number and the set of theories it involves about reincarnation and past lives, but if you do care to speculate about such matters, you can find your Life Purpose number easily enough, by adding your Expression and your Life Path numbers. Then, compare this number with the other numbers in your chart to see where and in what ways you are following your spiritual instincts, and where and how you are choosing not to listen to your inner voice.

Now that you have learned about all the numbers in your chart, you may or may not be satisfied with the results. Would you like to be more sensitive, artistic, self-assured, or forceful than your chart indicates? Well, while you can't do anything about your birth date, you can certainly change your name. By changing your name from what is on your birth certificate you won't change your basic personality, but you *can* change some things about yourself, and the results can be very effective. Many actors and actresses change their names, just as they may also change their appearances by having their hair professionally styled, their teeth straightened, or their figures slimmed down. In one sense all of this is superficial—the actor's essence remains unchanged. Yet the new image he projects often enables him to achieve things that might have been impossible for him in his original state.

So it may be a good idea to change your name. But don't do it impulsively or just for kicks some time when you're bored, because the result is bound to be somewhat disruptive—imagine having to get your driver's license, tax records, and credit cards all altered to show your new name! Be sure that making the change is really important to you, and that you can reasonably expect to be changing for the better.

CHAPTER III

the numbers in love

FOR MOST OF US, THERE ARE MANY SEEMingly unanswerable questions and problems surrounding the age-old question of love. What can you do to make your romantic life happier? How can you avoid disappointment?

Will everything in your life be all right if you can find the one perfect partner, a soul mate who understands and can satisfy all your needs and desires? When a relationship fails, do you blame yourself? Your partner? Circumstances or meddling in-laws?

More and more people are turning to numerology to help them find happiness in love with a soul mate whose combination of numbers is harmonious with their own. For these people, and for you, there can be such a thing as "living happily ever after." Numerology can help you make the most of any relationship, or gain wisdom from past failures so as to avoid repeating your mistakes.

In any romantic situation, the science of numbers

can help. As you have seen in Chapter II, numerology points not to one magic number that will show you the man or woman of your romantic dreams, but rather to a multitude of numerological possibilities that could lead to love. Each person is a combination of factors which in and of themselves are not necessarily harmonious and which respond in various ways—some of them positive and some destructive—to the individual's life experiences. What's important to keep in mind is not the inherent good or bad qualities of any number or combination of numbers, but how they compare with your own numbers and what both of you can do to help make the numbers add up to romantic bliss. As the saying goes, "nobody's perfect," but the numbers will show you how to work with your imperfections and strengths—as well as those of your mate—to find and keep happiness in love.

It's with this in mind that you can look to numerology to help you find a compatible mate, mend an ailing relationship, tell you the strengths and weaknesses of a particular partnership, or—if worse comes to worst—advise you if a certain relationship is hopeless and you should stop wasting time and emotional energy on it. This chapter will not explore what factors in a numerology chart, your own or someone else's, could make all relationships difficult. Instead, it is devoted to helping you gain a deeper understanding of individual personalities and how they relate to each other. In this chapter we will consider elements that specifically affect the compatibility between two charts.

The first factor may seem almost too ridiculously

simple: Even numbers and odd numbers are generally incompatible. The even numbers tend to be partnership minded, and a chart heavy in even numbers indicates a person to whom relationships are very important. Six is the number most favorable for close relationships, and a name or birth date with a 6 in it immediately suggests a person who gravitates toward commitment in love. A chart without a 6, on the other hand, most likely belongs to someone who either has never had a serious romance, or who has hopped from one romance to another trying to find the perfect partner. Likewise with the number 2. Those whose names or birth dates contain a 2 tend to think always of their partner's needs, even to the point where they forget their own. But people whose charts lack the accommodating 2 never see themselves as half of a pair, whether they're married or single. Instead, they think in terms of what's best for them alone, rather than for the couple. Naturally, these difficulties can be overcome—and will have a greater or lesser impact depending upon which numbers (Soul Urge, Latent number, Expression, Life Path, or Life Purpose) show such a compatibility or incompatibility—but the first step is realizing that they exist.

To the odd numbers, relationships are not nearly as important as to the even numbers. They are individualists, from self-involved 1, to creative 3, to freedom-loving 5, scholarly 7, and universalist 9. If odd numbers are prominent in your numerology chart, or in the chart of someone you're interested in, this doesn't mean that there will necessarily be problems in relationships. Not at all! The important thing is to find someone who shares your views and allows you space for developing your individual talents—while you, in turn, do the same for your partner. If you are spiritual, loving 7, for instance, or impersonal, universal 9, seek out a person whose numbers share your somewhat distanced outlook on life, not one whose chart shows a highly emotive, passionate personality.

Often it happens that when comparing your chart with that of several prospective lovers it's impossible to tell which one would be best. Remember that in most comparisons there are both negative and positive factors. If you find that you can't weigh one against the other and come up with an answer you're sure is right, don't be surprised. In many cases even the most experienced numerologist would be unable to decide which of two people whose charts are reasonably harmonious to your own is the one and only, absolutely perfect Mr. or Ms. Right. Probably you could be equally happy with both, though in different ways. Which one you eventually choose may depend more on circumstances than anything else. Absolute compatibility evolves more from working hard and responsibly with the numbers your chart and your mate's reflect. Revel in your harmonious area; be conscious of problem spots, and work to make them better. True, you may be lucky enough to discover that the person you're interested in really *is* an ideal partner. But such a clear-cut indication is the exception, not the rule. Happiness truly *is* in the numbers; you just have to know how to read them.

Another factor that is important in compatibility

is timing. Life goes through cycles, numerologically speaking, and this means that what you want in love at one time could be quite different from what you desire at another time. You may have heard people say they're separating or divorcing because they "outgrew each other" or "developed in different ways" as they got older. Likewise, the boy or girl next door who seemed to be nothing more than a pest a few years ago could come back and sweep you off your feet when the time is right.

Charting life cycles is not difficult. Since numerology is based on the numbers 1 through 9, not surprisingly the cycles are charted in nine-year spans. The first year of each cycle is a time of beginnings, of making adjustments to new circumstances; this is often a very favorable time for starting a relationship or entering into a marriage. The succeeding years in the cycle show the development of whatever you have initiated, with the ninth year being a time of completion. Romantically speaking, the ninth year can be a time when a romance moves from one phase to another, for instance, when you decide to end the courtship period and plan a wedding (preferably in the next year, the first year of the succeeding cycle). Or, at this juncture, or time of endings, you may decide to end a relationship that has proven to be unsatisfactory.

The first number involved in charting your cycles is 36 (4 x 9). It covers the four stages of development: infancy, childhood, adolescence, and young adulthood. By subtracting the number of your Life Path from 36 you get the number of years you will be under the influence of the first cycle, or First Pinnacle, as it is known. Then, to find out which number governs this cycle, add the digit of the month and the digit of the day of your birth date.

As an example, let's take the birth date February 14, 1956. This person's Life Path number is:

2 + 1 + 4 + 1 + 9 + 5 + 6 =
28 = 2 + 8 = 10 = 1

Subtracting 1 from 36, we find that his First Pinnacle lasted from birth to age 35. Adding the month and day of birth, we discover that this First Pinnacle was governed by the number 7 (2 + 1 + 4).

The Second Pinnacle, covering the next nine years (in this case, the years between 35 and 44), is arrived at by adding the digit of the day and the digit of the year of birth. Thus, the Second Pinnacle is governed by the number 8 (1 + 4 + 1 + 9 + 5 + 6 = 26 = 2 + 6 = 8).

The Third Pinnacle, covering the next nine years (in this case, the years between 44 and 53), is arrived at by adding the numbers of the first two pinnacles. Thus, the Third Pinnacle is governed by the number 6 (7 + 8 = 15 = 1 + 5 = 6).

The Fourth Pinnacle governs the years from the end of the Third Pinnacle to the end of life (in this case from the age of 53 onward). The number of this Pinnacle is arrived at by adding the digit of the birth month and the digit of the birth year (2 + 1 + 9 + 5 + 6 = 23 = 2 + 3 = 5).

From these Pinnacles this person's entire life can be charted. His first thirty-five years, under the influence of scholarly, rather solitary 7, may have been spent in preparing himself for some technical field of work, while in his Second Pinnacle, governed by 8, the number of material success, he was rewarded with wealth and honor. This allowed him to relax and enjoy life with his family in his Third Pinnacle, as is indicated by marriage- and family-oriented 6. But lighthearted 5, governing his last Pinnacle, suggests that his declining years will be spent traveling. With this number's curiosity and interest in foreign cultures, he may retire with his family to Tibet or Malaysia instead of Florida. And there, he'll probably pursue some new hobby or interest he may not have had time for before.

As a romantic possibility this person would be a poor marriage bet in his youth. As you'll see in Chapter X, 7 is spiritual and basically solitary, avoiding all close contact, including romantic encounters. If he married young, the relationship would probably end in divorce. The Second Pinnacle is slightly more favorable for love, but 8, the governing number of this cycle, is more concerned with achievement and material success than with relationships. Although he may marry during this Pinnacle, it might very well be essentially a marriage of convenience. It's not until after the age of 44, in the Third Pinnacle, that the happy relationship, which has so far eluded him, is not only possible but likely. And the adventuresome 5 of his later years in no way precludes the continuation of a happy love life.

However, it is important to bear in mind that while the Pinnacle influences can help or hinder one's natural expression, they do not supersede it. Each person is born a certain type of individual—as shown by the numbers of the name (Soul Urge, Latent number, and Expression)—with a certain Life Path to pursue. In other words, if the person whose Pinnacles we have been charting has several accommodating 2s and marriage-minded 6s in his name, he will probably have many relationships, perhaps even marriages, even under the solitary 7 influence of his early years.

Thus you can see it's important to be aware of your cycles. Attractions that seem right at a particular time in your life may not be likely to prove satisfying on a permanent basis. Fortunately, numerology can help you see whether a romantic attraction is just a passing thing or a long-lasting possibility. Cycles will affect all relationships—from the initial tug on your heartstrings to more permanent relationships, even the happiest of which have their ups and downs. At times, one partner or both may be more absorbed in other interests, such as building a career, than in love. And, of course, these cycles must be judged against the background of the relationship in general. For instance, in a 6 cycle a compatible partnership will bloom and even a difficult one will be a little easier to bear. On the other hand, during a 6 cycle even a person not usually interested in relationships will be "in the mood for love"—a feeling that unfortunately may fade once the cycle ends, perhaps leaving him or her stuck in a marriage that now has little appeal.

It would be impossible to chart all combinations of name numbers, Life Path numbers, and Pinnacle numbers, and explain how each will influence the others. This can only be done on an individual basis by a personal numerologist. But this book can show you how to be your own numerologist. By carefully studying the following chapters, which describe the meanings of the numbers, and trying to fit them into the appropriate slots in your own or someone else's numerology chart, you'll be amazed at the insight the numbers will yield. If the results puzzle and confuse you, don't be dismayed. People are infinitely complex and it is seldom possible to pigeonhole them neatly! When you have practiced on several charts, however, you should be able to detect some general trends which will help you understand yourself and others better—and help you choose more wisely in romantic matters.

CHAPTER IV

NUMBER 1

"THE ONE AND ONLY." HOW MANY TIMES have we heard that phrase used to indicate something unique, and special, not easily duplicated? That's the way 1 thinks of him or herself: special, different, not part of the crowd. Individualistic and independent, aggressive, bold, and inventive, your tendency always is to move ahead, to assume a leadership position in whatever situation you find yourself in. Although you are not unfriendly, you do not actively seek friends, since you are not dependent either for ideas or emotional support on other people. You have your own agenda, and you carry it forward with little concern for what others want or need. Cooperation is not natural to you. Waiting for others to make up their minds or to agree with your point of view would, you feel, inhibit the free flow of your originality.

You are capable of great achievements in areas where courage, boldness, initiative, and aggressiveness are required. You seek challenges and try to turn them into opportunities to do something new, different, or never before attempted. Naturally, with all your assets for moving ahead quickly, you are an activist who keeps things stirred up around you. But you're not just running around in circles: You tend to be single-minded and goal-oriented, with clearly defined objectives. So you're likely to be an achiever, whether it be on a broad scale or in a small area of concentration.

For all your ambitions, however, chances are you don't talk much about your plans, you just plunge in and start moving. And that's all for the best, because not only are you proud and resentful of criticism, but you often don't want advice of any kind and you tend to ignore it when it is offered. The idea of discussing your plans and making adjustments to keep in line with other people's suggestions would be quite unnatural for you. Basically you're a loner, knowing what you want and how you want to go about getting it. You want to be free to move ahead quickly, to explore, experiment, and pioneer, and you can't be bothered with waiting for slower people to catch up with you. Similarly, you tend to avoid situations where you have to submit your ideas to a committee and argue its members into doing things your way. Though you might eventually win the argument, you would regret the time and energy spent getting to that point.

With your initiative, inventiveness, and other leadership qualities you could easily become the head of a business organization, or have a business of your own. Whatever the particular framework, you would definitely have to be the leader. And since you dislike dealing with details, you'll need associates subordinate to you so you can delegate minor chores to them. The company president or project director who stares out the window all day formulating big plans is your ideal image of the way to go, though in reality you may have to deal with a lot of the nitty-gritty work on your projects. But that's all right as long as it's *your own* plans you're carrying out—in your own way.

While all this aggressive independence is fine for getting ahead in a career, it's not as helpful for the close relationships, including marriage. The concept of equality, of two more or less equal partners—in romance and all other areas—is contrary to your nature. Whether male or female, you want to be the boss in any relationship. If your partner is willing to take a subordinate role—your romance might very well flourish and then again, it might not. You can be selfish and self-absorbed, and so busy "looking out for number 1" that your lover's needs may be ignored if he or she doesn't fight for them. If your partner gives in all the time, you may become bored, while if he or she doesn't give in, you'll often tire of the constant conflict. Either way, not being emotionally dependent on others, you might easily walk out of a relationship. If things aren't working out to suit you, you're just as willing to be a loner in romance as in other areas.

Nevertheless, there are some people with whom you are naturally compatible: the odd numbers, excepting another 1, with whom there may be too much of a struggle for leadership, are all a fair bet.

Expressive 3; 5, who shares your love of freedom; 7, who shares your loner tendencies; and 9, who shares your large-scale ideas and attitudes. All have some affinity with you.

Of the even numbers, accommodating 2 and serene 6 might be the kind who'll be willing to give in to you, if you want to dominate in a relationship. However, you'd have little harmony with materialistic 4 or 8; they think in practical, rather impersonal terms while your leanings are very personal. Perhaps your best choice would be one of the odd numbers which indicate people who are individualistic, as you are, but in a different area from you, so they can do their own thing yet not be in conflict with you while you're following your path.

All of the foregoing is written as if there were such a thing as a "number 1 person." But actually, there isn't. Besides the various numbers in each name, there are five special numbers: Soul Urge, Latent, Expression, Life Path, and Life Purpose numbers. (Refer to Chapter II if you need to refresh your memory on what each of these numbers means and how they are derived.) Thus, the preceding description is actually of the number 1 itself, not of any specific type of person, and the qualities delineated apply wherever a 1 appears in your numerology chart. However, if this number holds one of the special positions in your chart, there are slight variations to the 1 qualities, as follows:

If 1 is your Soul Urge: You want to be a leader, originator, activator, and creator, to do everything in an individualistic way. You want to be known as a take-charge sort of person whose ideas are immediately accepted by everyone around you, so that as soon as you become involved in a group activity you start running it. Ideally, you want to meet obstacles and competition honestly and forthrightly, to overcome them with your courage and ability. Improving your skills and showing them off to advantage so they will be noticed and admired is part of your ideal vision of yourself. With this kind of inner motivation you tend to be an achiever, and you *will* be if circumstances permit. But there is a danger with a 1 Soul Urge: If the rest of your chart doesn't give you the ability or the opportunity to carry out your dreams, you may rush off in all the wrong directions, refusing to listen to advice or to adjust your activities to fit your overall situation. Or, you may become a petty tyrant—domineering, unreasonable, and arrogant—refusing to cooperate and insisting that if you can't have your own way you won't play.

If 1 is your Latent number: You see yourself as bold and adventurous, an admired leader exploring regions where no one else has ever been and meeting challenges that would daunt most other people. Whether or not you are able to put such ideas into action, however, depends on the rest of your chart, since Latent numbers in and of themselves have no power to act.

If 1 is your Expression number: A strong drive for independence and individuality makes you try to be a leader in anything you do. At your best you are courageous and determined, able to make plans and carry them out with overwhelming energy and resourcefulness. Because of this you are well-suited to start a business of your own, but it should be one that relies on your personal abilities and allows you to express your originality. If for any reason it's not feasible to have a business of your own, you will strive to express your individuality and initiative in some other way. And you *should* strive for this, since you could never be happy as a follower. You were meant to blaze paths for others to follow while you yourself keep forging ahead constantly into new areas.

If 1 is your Life Path number: Life will keep bringing you opportunities to be a leader and an innovator, and it is up to you to capitalize on these opportunities. If your Soul Urge or Expression number is 1, or if there is at least one 1 letter in your name (A, J, or S), you'll have no problem moving ahead with your plans. Lacking either of these, you will have to put to work whatever personality assets your chart does contain in order to take advantage of the chances for leadership.

If 1 is your Life Purpose number: This number represents the sum total of your personality and your life experiences. With 1 in this position, you were meant to be an individualist and a ground-breaker. Using whatever assets the rest of your numerology chart shows, you are expected to try as hard as you can to leave a personal imprint on the world in some way—most often in the form of a pioneering effort which affects not only yourself but many others as well.

CHAPTER V

NUMBER 2

AS THE NUMBER 1 IS THE EPITOME OF INdividuality, 2 is the essence of partnership and cooperation. You are a follower rather than a leader, receptive rather than aggressive—sensitive, helpful, considerate, tactful, patient, and understanding. You have no desire to dominate others, and in fact you see no need for domination on either side because you feel that all differences can be resolved through compromise. Other people can grab the spotlight while you are content to remain quietly in the background, using your tact and diplomacy to keep things running smoothly for others. Yet for you, to give to others is like receiving a gift. And because you give freely and happily, the publicity and fame you do not actively seek for yourself often comes to you anyway, seemingly by accident.

You have an excellent sense of rhythm, timing, and color. And because of this, music, dance, fashion design, interior decorating, or anything else along those lines would be occupations well-suited to you. But whether or not you are actually involved in the arts, either as a profession or an avocation, they hold a strong appeal for you, with music being your special favorite. If you have talent you will want to develop it, both for your own enjoyment and to give pleasure to others. But in order to attain any notable success you would probably need a sponsor or agent, since you lack the competitiveness and ruthlessness to push yourself ahead. Even if you have no particular talent of your own, in all probability you genuinely admire those who do. And with your other-directed nature, you can be the world's greatest appreciator; you can sincerely and without jealousy be a patron of the arts and a helper to any performer who seems to need you.

Naturally, with your cooperative, unselfish attitude, you tend to attract all sorts of people, of both sexes. You have many friends, not all of whom share the same attitudes and opinions, so you may often find yourself acting as a peacemaker or negotiator between two conflicting friends. This pleases you, because you always want to be surrounded by an atmosphere of affection and harmony, and helping to achieve such an ambience is one of your goals in life. In this effort you may even tell little white lies, if that's necessary to keep the peace and avoid hurting anyone. Though you love to gossip with friends, you can be very subtle and discreet. People can safely tell you their deepest secrets, knowing you will not repeat them.

As receptivity is a part of your nature, so, too, is

accumulation. You allow things to come to you, and they do. Small things are your special favorites, and chances are that you have a collection of some sort—probably miniature items such as stamps or pillboxes. You also like to accumulate detailed facts and odd bits of information. A perpetual student, your mental reference file is crammed with trivia. You are interested in details and are careful, patient, and efficient in dealing with them. This talent, added to your willingness to stay in the background and subordinate your own interests to those of others, often makes you the perfect assistant to an executive, able to supply sympathy, support, or information as needed. Though not aggressive, you can be patiently persistent and gently persuasive. Thus, you are the power behind the throne in more ways than one.

Subtly accumulating power, though, is not your agenda. Rather, what you want and greatly need is love, affection, and a deep emotional rapport with others. It would not embarrass you to be told that you are a soft touch or that you fall in love too easily and indiscriminately; instead, you wish everyone else were as responsive. You also wish that they shared your desire to please and to put your partner's needs before your own. Unfortunately, not everyone does, so you run the risk of being exploited by more selfish people.

Your compliant, giving attitude can also create other problems for you. For example, you may become almost a doormat, always letting others have their way for fear of creating conflict or offending them and thereby losing the love and protection you so greatly desire. Or you may totally surrender your individuality and any definite purpose in life to your lover, and just drift along trying to be whatever your current partner wants you to be.

The people who are most likely to take advantage of you are the self-involved odd numbers. Highly individualistic 1 could use your willing service without appreciating it. Similarly, rather superficial 3, freedom-loving 5, and universalist 9 lack the depth of feeling that would satisfy you in a romantic partner. And scientific 7 is uncomfortable with your demonstrative affection.

Your best bet for finding the cooperation and harmony you seek is 6, which is as partnership-minded as you are. Materialistic 4 and 8 might be a little cool emotionally, but they can make you feel protected, and will work hard to be good providers. You appreciate this; and anyway, you have enough love for two! While you don't insist on wealth and luxury, you do like a certain amount of comfort, ease, and freedom from financial worries.

All of the foregoing is written as if there were such a thing as a "number 2 person." But actually, there isn't. Besides the various numbers in each name, there are five special numbers: Soul Urge, Latent, Expression, Life Path, and Life Purpose numbers. (Refer to Chapter II if you need to refresh your memory on what each of these numbers means and how they are derived.) Thus, the preceding description is actually of the number 2 itself, not of any specific type of person, and the qualities delineated apply wherever a 2 appears in your numerology chart. However, if this number holds one of the special positions in your chart, there are slight variations in the 2 qualities, as follows:

If 2 is your Soul Urge: A desire for peace, harmony, love, and comfort motivates you. You have no urge to remake the world or start anything new, to shine in public or achieve great things. Instead, your personal vision is of a cultured, conflict-free atmosphere where everyone gets along with everyone else. The perfect partner, you prefer to follow rather than to lead, and you want to devote your energies to maintaining a harmonious atmosphere in your relationships. There is no compulsiveness in the things you demand of yourself. You have no particular desire to be wealthy or successful; you just want to be loved, happy, and comfortable. Unfortunately, this lack of ambitious drive, combined with your compliant attitude, could prevent you from developing any talents you happen to have and inhibit achievement of any definite purpose in life. You may also become dependent and fearful, and thus easily exploited.

If 2 is your Latent number: You see yourself as a very loving, giving person, willing to remain in the background, unobtrusively helping others while asking nothing for yourself in return. Whether or not you are actually as self-effacing as you inwardly feel, however, depends on the rest of your chart, since the Latent numbers in themselves have no power to act.

If 2 is your Expression number: Your strength lies in your ability to work well with people, to be a peacemaker, a diplomat, and an expert at constructive compromise. An atmosphere of ease and comfort is important to you; without it you feel adrift, helpless, and somewhat inclined toward self-pity. In a difficult situation you look for someone to protect you and fight your battles. Fortunately, you can probably always find someone willing to do that, since your compliant, cooperative attitude brings you many friends. Very emotional and affectionate, you fall in love easily and would be unhappy without marriage or some other long-term romantic arrangement in your life. In business, you prefer to work in a group or with a committee, or at least have a partner.

If 2 is your Life Path number: You will have many opportunities for selfless service, and will be expected to give affection, understanding, sympathy, and help without thought of reward for yourself. Nevertheless, as you give so shall you receive, since you'll have many loyal friends who support you, fight for you, and see to it that your kindnesses are repaid. If your Soul Urge or Expression number is 2, or if there is at least one 2 letter in your name (B, K, or T), you'll have no problem following this path. However, lacking either of these, you may have to learn to be patient and cooperative, and to subdue selfish ambitions for these will cause you to fail.

If 2 is your Life Purpose number: This number represents the sum total of your personality and your life experiences. With 2 in this position, you were meant to bring peace and harmony to as much of the world around you as you are able to influence. It is through giving that you achieve personal success, and your unselfish service may have much broader consequences than even you realize.

CHAPTER VI

NUMBER 3

CREATIVE, VERSATILE, AMUSING, AND ALways young at heart, you take whatever life brings your way, never allowing yourself to become depressed, worried, or discouraged. Life is a game to you—and you'd like to make it a game for everyone else as well. A natural entertainer, you are interested in everything, and you try to convey your enthusiasm to others. A happy, extroverted person, you like to tell funny stories and keep all your listeners in a good mood. Naturally, this makes you a sought-after party guest, which pleases you, because being popular and favorably noticed is one of your major goals. Like an actor, you feel you're always on stage, and you'd be hurt and disappointed if you were ignored. You consciously seek the spotlight. Fortunately your innate good taste, love of beauty, and genuine lust for life lead you to use uplifting, amusing, and captivating ways of attracting attention, which others find quite pleasing.

Words, written or spoken, attract you, and you

have a natural talent for expressing yourself through writing, teaching, and acting. Imaginative and creative, you can find innovative or artistic ways to convey your thoughts and feelings. And though you tend to be casual about most things, you'll probably be willing to go to considerable trouble to improve your communication talents. You may take classes in acting or public speaking, writing or copyediting, for example. Or you'll make a conscious effort to enlarge your vocabulary or your collection of funny stories. Instinctive actor that you are, you might also practice dramatic gestures in front of your mirror. But there's a negative side to all this: If you talk too much, you may bore or antagonize people, or let slip things about them that were told you in confidence. Also, with your inordinate faith in the power of words, you tend to admire people who can talk themselves out of tight spots, and you underestimate those who are more deserving but less articulate. Your judgment of people is sometimes badly mistaken or based on superficialities.

Nevertheless, your cheerful disposition and childlike enjoyment of life make your faults easy to forgive. You want to be popular, and undoubtedly most people like you as much as you like them. Subtlety and deviousness don't come naturally to you. You especially enjoy children and animals because of the simplicity of your own nature, which echoes theirs.

Because you want your world to be as beautiful as you can make it, you tend to ornament and beautify everything around you. And you are versatile and talented enough to be skilled in many forms of artistic creativity. The trouble is you may scatter your talents so widely that you never actually achieve anything substantial. You are a clever jack-of-all-trades, but not a significant achiever. This bothers you less than it might bother other people, however; you're more concerned with having fun in the present than with leaving a solid imprint on the future.

Naturally, in all your partying and socializing you make friends with members of the opposite sex, and you enjoy that. Flirting is one of the things you do for fun, but usually it doesn't mean much—although a jealous partner might not understand this! It's your nature to be charming and complimentary to everyone, but you don't lie and pretend to be more in love than you actually are: You tend to be loyal to your friends and faithful in your romantic commitments. When you are really in love, your lover will certainly know about it. With your talent for expressing yourself in words, chances are you won't stop with a simple "I love you." You'll be writing long notes, or even poems or songs, to your beloved.

As a romantic partner you are bested suited to 1, who can match your enthusiasm for life and all its possibilities. Variety-loving 5 and universalist 9 also make good matches. The one odd number that doesn't suit you is 7, which is as shy and withdrawn as you are sociable.

With the even numbers 2 and 6—which like people and are as eager to form relationships as you are—you could have some rapport. On the other hand, 2 is too heavily emotional to please you and will probably be inclined to resent the way you scatter your attention and smiles all around a room. Likewise, 6 is too serious, responsible, and family-oriented to be your best choice in love; 6 would soon be trying to induce you to settle down and cope with children and mortgages. And hardworking, ambitious 4 and 8 types are the kind who simply wouldn't understand you; they would consider your fun-loving ways frivolous, and would soon become impatient with your impracticality and your refusal to get really serious about making and saving money.

All of the foregoing is written as if there were such a thing as a "number 3 person." But actually, there isn't. Besides the various numbers in each name, there are five special numbers: Soul Urge, Latent, Expression, Life Path and Life Purpose numbers. (Refer to Chapter II if you need to refresh your memory on what each of these numbers means and how they are derived.) Thus, the preceding description is actually of the number 3 itself, not of any specific type of person, and the qualities delineated apply wherever a 3 appears in your numerology chart. However, if this number holds one of the special positions in your chart, there are slight variations in the 3 qualities, as follows:

If 3 is your Soul Urge: Though winning rewards is important to you, you want to succeed without working too hard. You like to think of yourself as having been born with so many talents that they automatically bubble out when you choose to use them. As a student, you want to come up with the right answers without having to study; in fact, with your glib talents, you may pretend you know answers when you don't. You are proud of your ability to deal with words, and you'll go to considerable lengths to develop and improve whatever skills you were born with. Friendship, love, and sociability are very important to you. Your ideal image of yourself includes being able to walk into a roomful of people secure in the knowledge that many of them know you and love you. And you get more pleasure from this personal, friendly reaction than you do from being greeted with a rather impersonal admiration for your achievements. With a 3 Soul Urge the danger lies in superficiality; in cultivating a glib, life-of-the-party image, you may fail to develop any of your other talents or work at sharing your childlike enjoyment of life.

If 3 is your Latent number: You see yourself as basically an artistic, creative person, popular and sought after. A welcome guest wherever you go, you shine before an appreciative audience, large or small as the case may be. You shed light and beauty all around you, both through creativity and through the happiness you bring to others.

If 3 is your Expression number: You are extroverted and versatile, entertaining and amusing. You want to be with people and make them laugh. With your gift for self-expression, you have a wonderful way with words, both written and spoken. There is something youthful about your personality, and you show the imagination, freshness, and spontaneity of a child. Like a child, too, you deal in terms of the here and now, with little thought for yesterday or tomorrow. Your attention span is short. You have plenty of ideas for starting things but don't plan ahead, so you may fail by not following through on projects you've begun. This may be aggravated if you can't learn to channel your many talents or develop them enough to make them useful.

If 3 is your Life Path number: You will have many opportunities to express yourself before an audience, either personally or through your artistic creations. The lighter, more decorative aspects of life are your area of operation, and you should strive to beautify and embellish everything you touch. Sociability is also important to you, and you should learn to dress well and speak fluently so you can present yourself attractively at all times, and before any kind of an audience. If your Soul Urge or Expression number is 3, or if there is at least one 3 letter in your name (C, L, or U) you'll have no problem establishing yourself. Lacking either of these, you will have to make an effort to cultivate your artistic talents and learn to project a charming, carefree image that will win you popularity.

If 3 is your Life Purpose number: This number represents the sum total of your personality and your life experiences. With 3 in this position, you were meant to bring happiness, art, and beauty to the world around you. Yet you should not be content with being a likable dilettante; you must develop and use your talents responsibly, not scatter them carelessly and waste your time in idleness.

CHAPTER VII

NUMBER 4

STRONG AND STABLE, PRACTICAL, DEpendable, and conscientious, you are happiest when you can run your life so that everything is orderly and well-regulated, based on logic and common sense. In spite of any obstacles that may arise, you strive to carry out the plans you've made, to keep your promises and fulfill all your obligations carefully. With your strong sense of duty you try to finish whatever you have taken on, and you never take the easiest way out if you encounter difficulties. You pride yourself on your endurance and self-discipline, and you want to do things in what you consider the right way, regardless of how much effort it takes. You believe strongly in rules and regulations, and in upholding traditional standards—even if everyone else you know is ignoring them!

Obviously, you make many demands on yourself, but you don't think of this as being especially praiseworthy. You dislike boasting, in yourself or in others, feeling that if you do your duty conscientiously your work will speak for itself. Honesty is among the virtues you cherish. You try to view yourself realistically and dislike pretense, insincerity, or fuzzy-headed thinking in others. You like to think of yourself as being clear-eyed, sensible, and practical, with your feet on the ground at all times. Logical, analytical, and precise, you want to deal with facts only. In all things you demand proof, and scorn the idea of taking anything on faith. Imagination and creativity are not your major assets, but you don't really miss having them. Conservative in your viewpoint, you prefer to operate along traditional, well-established paths rather than experiment in new areas or try out new methods of expression.

Your standards tend to be material ones. You strive to handle financial matters prudently and to be cautious and economical with money. In your eyes, that which is useful has more value than that which is merely ornamental. You would feel guilty about buying something you didn't need simply because it was pretty. In this way you often deny yourself pleasure, but this doesn't bother you. A firm, and even rigid, self-disciplinarian, you set yourself limits according to your standards of how life should be lived, and you take pride in adhering to those standards. Unfortunately, you also try to apply these limitations and standards to other people with whom you are involved, and this sometimes makes you very unpopular. If you have children, they may feel you are lacking in warmth and understanding, and are repressing their individuality. Likewise, your subordinates at work may find you unpleasantly rigid. As for business associates on or above your own level, you may complain if you find that they fail to meet your standards. While this may not make you popular, you yourself will probably be satisfied that you did your duty as you saw it.

But you are not simply trying to make other people—or yourself—unhappy by your rigidity. Rather, you are motivated by a strong urge to build something solid, substantial, and enduring. This can be a project of physical substance, such as a building. Or, it can be a business you have started, a fortune to be passed on to your family, or ideas and theories in some practical area such as economics. Yours is a nature that thinks in terms not only of today, but of yesterday—drawing on its traditions and achievements—and tomorrow, because of the lasting impact of what you have accomplished. And because of the value and permanence of this vision you feel that the self-limitation and self-discipline you impose on yourself and others is worthwhile.

Unfortunately, your friends and co-workers often don't see it that way. Your sternly austere attitude may make you repel love or friendship even though you very much want and need them. Although you may want to be friendly, you'll often find yourself unable to relax enough to form relationships with people who don't conform to your standards. Or you may find them simply silly, extravagant, disorganized, and impractical, with ideas so different from your own that it's impossible to find any common ground. On their side, you may seem stuffy, narrow-minded, rigid, or even just plain dull because of your inability to relax and have fun.

You would feel uneasy around the odd numbers, each of which in its own way is antagonistic to the rules and traditions you live by. And, in turn, they would tend to see your more negative characteristics. Pioneering 1, creative 3, and variety-loving 5 would dislike your rigidity, lack of imagination, and failure to seek enjoyment out of life. Studious 7 and cause-oriented 9 would find your materialistic values wrong, feeling that your achievements, however worthy, are not human-oriented enough.

Because of the firmness with which you adhere to your ideas, another 4, who is bound to share the substance of those ideas although perhaps in a somewhat different form, could be very compatible with you. Also, gentle 2 could soften your rigidity, if you didn't try to overpower this accommodating type. Responsible 6 might meet your standards and, again, provide a softening influence. And an 8 could match you in material talents, and also teach you a lot about broadening your horizons and rising above the merely routine. With any of these compatible numbers your solid dependability and desire always to do the right, honorable thing could provide adequate compensation for your self-restraint and unemotional outlook on life and love.

All of the foregoing is written as if there were such a thing as a "number 4 person." But actually, there isn't. Besides the various numbers in each name, there are five special numbers: Soul Urge, Latent, Expression, Life Path, and Life Purpose numbers.

(Refer to Chapter II if you need to refresh your memory on what each of these numbers means and how they are derived.) Thus, the preceding description is actually of the number 4 itself, not of any specific type of person, and the qualities delineated apply wherever a 4 appears in your numerology chart. However, if this number holds one of the special positions in your chart, there are slight variations in the 4 qualities, as follows:

If 4 is your Soul Urge: Your ideal image of yourself is of someone honest, loyal, dependable, sensible, and well organized—the type of person without whom society could not operate or law and order be maintained. You have a strong sense of duty, and you take pride in exercising the endurance and self-discipline necessary to accomplish whatever you feel is part of your obligation to your job, your family, and the society in which you live. The rules and regulations and the orderly routines by which you live—which might seem so tiresome to a different type of person—make you feel comfortable and secure. You admire achievements and traditions that have outlasted passing fads, and you hope to add some enduring achievement of your own to the world. The possible danger associated with a 4 Soul Urge is that you may become too narrow-minded, rule bound, and intolerant of change. You may make too many unreasonable demands and impose too many limitations on yourself and others.

If 4 is your Latent number: You see yourself as a solid, conservative person, a pillar of the community—orderly, well organized, precise, well focused. Hard work is the avenue by which you win appreciation and recognition, and you handle all your affairs in a very practical, profitable way. A good financial manager, you are cautious with your money, and not prone to throwing it around or taking big risks.

If 4 is your Expression number: Endurance and reliability are among your prime characteristics, and you can be counted on to dig in and see a task through to the end. A good organizer and a hard worker, you're careful with money and are always around when needed; you are one of the solid builders of the world. You long for affection and friendship but your austere attitude and rigid view of life limit the number of people with whom you can get along. Certainly you are not the kind who considers the world well lost for love. You would not accept a romantic partner who was beneath you, socially or economically, or break the rules of conventional respectability for love's sake.

If 4 is your Life Path number: You were meant for a life of practical achievement, hard work, discipline, and endurance. You will have many opportunities to build structures of lasting benefit for all and to teach others the value and gratification of realistic accomplishment. Your path is materialistic, fact-oriented, and down to earth. It may also be difficult and limited in scope until you learn to transcend the limitations imposed on you by your life circumstances. If your Soul Urge or Expression number is 4, or if there is at least one 4 letter in your name (D, M, or V) you'll be able to more freely follow your path of practical achievement.

Lacking either of these, however, you may have to find ways to rise above limitations or handicaps to achieve the major successes of which 4 is capable.

If 4 is your Life Purpose number: This number represents the sum total of your personality and your life experiences. With 4 in this position, you were meant to work hard, building not just for the moment but for the future as well, so as to be able to leave behind some worthwhile and permanent achievements. Your life may not be an easy one, but your influence on the world can be significant in the long run.

CHAPTER VIII

NUMBER 5

CHANGE, VARIETY, FREEDOM, ADVENTURE, and travel are the things you love. So when it comes to rules, limitations, conventions, or responsibilities you do your best to avoid them. To you the security of a routine, no matter how luxurious and comfortable it might be, is like being stuck in a muddy rut. But fear not. Actually, you are unlikely to be stuck anywhere long, since your tendency is to initiate change. Somehow or other, you always manage to stir things up and give them a fresh vitality. Not only do you enjoy variety, and even turmoil, for their own sake, but you know instinctively that your best opportunities come from situations that are in motion.

Quick to think and act, versatile and opportunistic, you are able to size up new circumstances and immediately see how they can be used to advantage. You have no respect for the argument that something should be done a certain way because it's always been done that way. If new methods seem more appropriate to any given situation, you are instantly ready to discard the old ways and make new adjustments. In fact, unless restrained you are sometimes accused of going too far and throwing out things that still have use and value. You may need to learn moderation in this respect if you are to show good judgment in deciding what to keep and what to discard. "Newer" isn't always synonymous with "better."

An adventurer and a nonconformist, you do not want to be bound by the rules or the ideas of other. Unconventional and extremely curious, you refuse to be a sheep politely following the herd. Rather, you want to see and experience as much of life as possible firsthand, and nothing would please you more than to have the freedom to take off for new territory at the drop of a hat, as the spirit moves you. Since your strong curiosity impels you to investigate, not just look at the surface of what you see, wherever you go you want to poke into everything. It's this poking around that motivates you to initiate change. Like the child continually asking, "Why, Daddy?" you stir people up and make them see that what they have been accepting unquestioningly for years is not necessarily right or reasonable. In this way you are a great factor for change, progress, and improvement in the world.

As has already been noted in this book, 5 is the number that turns up most often in numerology. It's rare to find a name that doesn't contain at least one 5. This is not surprising; since human beings have five senses, five fingers, five toes, etc., 5 is known as the "number of man." If 5 is strong in your chart, on one level you are content with being ordinary—the common man, as they say. On the other hand, you are actually quite uncommon in that you want to satisfy all your senses and experience life to the fullest in a very physical way, enjoying all its variety and pleasures. Not surprisingly, you enjoy the company of all kinds of people and you love being in crowds—mixing, mingling, and making friends. Almost any subject intrigues you: art, science, music, travel, sports, and everything else—especially if you're learning things that are new to you. You like to talk and, with your varied interests, you may very likely be a fascinating conversationalist. With you, being ordinary certainly doesn't equate with being dull.

Though not a scholarly type, your quick mind and lively curiosity may make you something of an intellectual. Yet basically you are physically oriented, and the so-called pleasures of the flesh—eating, drinking, and sex—have a strong appeal for you. In fact, you need to beware of overindulgence in these areas, and of simply having your fun and then moving on. You like people and mean no harm, but you may hurt them unwittingly unless you can learn to be loyal in both friendships and love. As a romantic partner you tend to be exciting and fun, but not necessarily reliable. With your love of freedom and dislike of routine, it isn't easy for you to commit to a permanent relationship, except perhaps with someone who shares your adventuresome spirit and who is willing to join you in your globe-trotting experiences.

Of the odd numbers, 1 and 3 exhibit some of

your own enjoyment of living, and you often get along famously with them. While 9's far-flung interests parallel your own, you don't share the strong 9 dedication to causes and helping people; but nonetheless, the two of you would certainly have a lot of experiences to enjoy together. Studious 7 would probably fascinate you with the depth of its thinking, but you want crowds and fun while 7 is serious minded and uncomfortable in crowds. Another 5 could be a good partner for you if you could both stop your restless movement long enough to get together.

As far as the even numbers are concerned, they have little appeal to you on a personal level. Even accommodating 2 and 6 wouldn't please you for long, 2 being too emotional and sentimental for your taste, and 6 being too responsible and stable. But it's 4 and 8 who really rub you the wrong way—straining your usually boundless desire to get along well with others. You would find it difficult to appreciate their material values, or to understand how they experience so much enjoyment from working hard and living within a framework of the established rules you so detest. The self-limitations and discipline of 4 and the putting off till a suitable time the fun you could be having today is the kind of mind-set you find infuriating.

All of the foregoing is written as if there were such a thing as a "number 5 person." But actually, there isn't. Besides the various numbers in each name, there are five special numbers: Soul Urge, Latent, Expression, Life Path, and Life Purpose numbers.

(Refer to Chapter II if you need to refresh your memory on what each of these numbers means and how they are derived.) Thus, the preceding description is actually of the number 5 itself, not of any specific type of person, and the qualities delineated apply wherever 5 appears in your numerology chart. However, if this number holds one of the special positions in your chart, there are slight variations on the 5 qualities, as follows:

If 5 is your Soul Urge: Pleasure, especially on the physical plane, is definitely on your mind, though the specific type of enjoyment you seek and how strenuously you pursue it will depend on the rest of your numerology chart. But whatever else you enjoy, you want to see and experience as much of life as possible. And in your ideal image of yourself you have the equipment for this: a quick mind, versatility, a talent for languages, and an ability to adapt to any situation or personality. You would like to have unlimited freedom and great variety in your life, as well as the opportunity to make progressive changes wherever you feel they are needed. You don't want to be bound by rules or other people's ideas, or to be tied down to routine and detail. If someone *does* try to rein you in, you see yourself as having the talent and ingenuity to get away. Unfortunately, that desire for independence and change can be pursued to the point where you refuse to stick long enough to any one thing to achieve a significant result. You often choose transitory pleasures rather than loyalty to any particular person, principle, or purpose. Overindulgence in physical pleasures—eating, drinking, sex, alcohol, or drugs—is another problem with a 5 Soul Urge.

If 5 is your Latent number: You see yourself as young at heart, happy, and free. You like to travel, and feel you can do so since you have no pressing responsibilities. Foreign countries, people, and customs appeal to you. You are open to new ideas and circumstances, to change and adventure, seeing all of these as ways to learn and grow. You consider yourself versatile, multitalented, and progressive in thought.

If 5 is your Expression number: A born innovator and instigator of change, versatile and opportunistic, you are quickly able to size up each new situation and see how it can be used to advantage. Friendly and sociable, you gravitate toward crowds and usually are able to adapt to and fit in with people of all types and cultures. You probably learn easily and may be particularly adept at languages because of your strong interest in travel and in the customs of other lands. Since you are interested in and curious about everything, you aim to have many experiences and to learn from all of them. Because of your delight in jumping from one thing to another you are sometimes accused of being too restless, or unreliable and irresponsible. To a certain extent this may be true, but you are also a potent factor for constructive change and progress in the world.

If 5 is your Life Path number: You were meant for a life of change, excitement, variety, and freedom. You will have many opportunities to travel and to have new experiences, learning from everyone you meet and everything you do. Versatility and adaptability are qualities you should cultivate because the unexpected will often crop up in your life, forcing you out of one set of circumstances into completely new ones. If your Soul Urge or Expression number is 5, or if there is at least one 5 in your name (E, N, or W), you will travel on your path of variety and change easily and unencumbered. Lacking either of these, you may have to invest extra effort in using the adaptability and versatility you *do* have to help you enjoy and promote change and progress. Don't strive to find a comfortable routine to settle in, for you'll only be shaken out of it sooner or later.

If 5 is your Life Purpose number: This number represents the sum total of your personality and your life experiences. With 5 in this position, you were meant to promote progressive change, not simply to stir things up for the fun of it. Though you are not particularly ambitious, you can inspire changes that carry a major influence on the world's history.

CHAPTER IX

NUMBER 6

A HAPPY HOME LIFE, LASTING RELATIONSHIPS, responsibility, and roots are what you long for. The number 6, often referred to as the "cosmic parent," relates to working with and for others, helping, advising, and comforting them. This is usually true on all levels—in your own family, in any social group with which you are involved, as well as in the community at large. Accepting responsibility for how the world is run comes naturally to you, and you benefit from the responsibilities you accept. The only thing you have to guard against is doing too much for others, taking on their problems as if they were your own. It is important that you stop short of this, so as to teach other people to handle their problems for themselves. In keeping with the idea of the cosmic parent, you express yourself most positively when you are able to let go, rather than try to live other people's lives for them.

Marriage is strongly related to this number, and

if 6 is prominent in your numerology chart you may want to get married at an early age. But since 6 is also concerned with other domestic responsibilities, you have the special ability to handle lovingly and without resentment such obligations as an aging parent, or a handicapped or foster child. If you are a single parent, and you marry someone with children of his or her own, you will be better suited than most to keep the arrangement harmonious and happy. You try very hard to show patience and good judgment in creating a balance between all who are in your domestic sphere. For to you, the happiness of the group is much more important than any one person's individual rights—including yours. And you're willing to work hard to keep the household on a fair, happy, even keel.

All this effort seems worthwhile and even necessary, because you're not one of those whose love story ends at the altar. To you, the wedding ceremony is just the beginning of the fulfilling domesticity you've been planning practically since you were born. You don't enjoy being alone, and marriage suits you perfectly because it makes you part of a permanent twosome. And while others may enter marriage with the thought of divorce if it doesn't work out, this is hardly true of you. Marriage is a lifelong commitment you take seriously. Nor would a relationship outside of marriage suit your basically conservative nature unless you felt it would lead to marriage.

Once you have a home of your own, you try to make it as attractive to look at as it is harmonious to be in. You love to be surrounded by art, culture, beauty, ease, and comfort, and as soon as you take up residence anywhere you set about the delightful task of trying to make your domestic surroundings meet your standards. Of all the arts, your special love is music, and no doubt you'll have the most elaborate electronic sound equipment you can afford, or perhaps a piano or some other musical instrument. Those Victorian pictures of smiling families clustered around pianos singing together don't seem hopelessly old-fashioned to you; more likely, they seem to epitomize all the joys of domesticity you are hoping to create for yourself and your own family.

Naturally, with all the emphasis you place on commitment and domesticity, adjustment, and harmony, you would make the perfect mate for the right person. But although you may be willing to subordinate your own ego to the needs of a partnership, not everyone else is willing to do the same. Individualistic 1 wouldn't dream of giving up his or her own desires for the good of the group, for instance, and a match with this number may be too emotionally taxing. Lighthearted 3 and 5 try to avoid responsibility and lack the stability you want. Also, you have a tendency to be conservative in viewpoint in order to protect the established group values you so cherish, while 5 is as dedicated to changing these traditions as you are to maintaining them. With withdrawn, very private 7 your nest-building instincts are totally incompatible. Universalist 9, on the other hand, shares your concern for others and might even benefit you by directing your attention to more broad areas than your own home;

but be careful on the home front, for 9 might not want to be confined to your smaller world.

A relationship with accommodating 2 or another 6 could be very happy. These pairs will have to work hard to add a touch of decisiveness to the relationship, however, to counteract the willingness to compromise that both of these numbers share. Stability and a sense of responsibility are as strong in 4 as they are in you; this rather rigid personality could use your softening influence, and while you find 4 a bit cold at times, basically this number is in line with your own principles. Materialistic 8 is more interested in money-making than in love, but this alliance should at least provide you with the kind of income that makes a beautiful home possible.

All of the foregoing is written as if there were such a thing as a "number 6 person." But actually, there isn't. Besides the various numbers in each name, there are five special numbers: Soul Urge, Latent, Expression, Life Path, and Life Purpose numbers. (Refer to Chapter II if you need to refresh your memory on what each of these numbers means and how they are derived.) Thus, the preceding description is actually of the number 6 itself, not of any specific type of person, and the qualities delineated apply wherever 6 appears in your numerology chart. However, if this number holds one of the special positions in your chart, there are slight variations on the 6 qualities, as follows:

If 6 is your Soul Urge: Strong feelings and a very personal attitude are what you like to see in yourself. You want to be concerned primarily with people, to be motivated by their needs. You want to be sympathetic toward everyone's problems and to raise the standard of living of the whole world. Furthermore, you assume it can be done by negotiation and adjustment, rather than through conflict. You believe in justice, and you are a strong advocate of laws designed to keep an equitable balance between opposing factions. On a personal level, your conventionality and love of hearth and home make you one of those who do not believe in taking love where you find it, without responsibility or commitments. Regardless of the social mores of your group, you want love to develop into a stable, settled arrangement, preferably marriage. But you must avoid becoming a household drudge if you marry, and must also try not to take on too much responsibility for others in your family. If you allow yourself to interfere too much in other people's lives, you could end up a gossip, busybody, or meddler. The harmonious balance you try to maintain in other areas of your life should also be applied to the way you help others.

If 6 is your Latent Number: You see yourself as the perfect center of the perfect family, full of peace, harmony, and love. Your beautiful, artistic home is warm with music and flowers, and the doors are always open to relatives and friends. Not only your family, but others too, come to you for advice and comfort, and you are always ready to oblige. Though your home is the center of your life, you are willing to help in whatever areas there is need.

If 6 is your Expression number: Cooperation, adjustment, and teamwork are your watchwords. Responsible and protective, you tend to take on the problems of others and to be free with advice and sympathy—admirable qualities as long as you can restrain yourself from meddling or from taking on too much of someone else's burden. A lover of peace and harmony, you tend to preserve a warm, affectionate, and personal atmosphere around you, both at home and elsewhere. Since your interests are centered around your home, a fulfilling domestic life is important to your happiness. With an Expression number of 6, which is related to marriage, you will certainly want to get married, probably at an early age, and if your first attempt doesn't turn out well you are likely to try again. It can be said to your credit that you will do more than your share to keep your home life serene, through your self-sacrificing sense of service and cooperation.

If 6 is your Life Path Number: You were meant to be a protector and preserver on a social level, promoting cooperation and harmony within your group. Life will bring you many opportunities to use your talents for helping and serving others, making adjustments or compromises, and assuming responsibility for the general welfare. Marriage is one of the special concerns of 6, and you will be interested in everything connected with personal relationships, your family, and your home. If your Soul Urge or Expression number is 6, or if there is at least one 6 letter in your name (F, O, or X), you will follow this path quite easily, reveling in your natural ability to help others. If, on the other hand, you lack either of these, you must cultivate a sense of responsibility toward your family and toward weaker members of society, such as children and the old. And if romantic relationships fail, you must strive to develop the cooperative, other-directed attitude that helps make them work.

If 6 is your Life Purpose number: This number represents the sum total of your personality and your life experiences. With 6 in this position, you can be a powerful force for peace in the world, both through what you yourself do and through the influence you spread in your family and in the social group to which you belong.

CHAPTER X

NUMBER 7

ONE THING THAT CAN'T BE SAID OF YOU is that you're ordinary, either in your goals or in your philosophy of life. You aspire to be a rare, special sort of individual, seeking wisdom, perfection, and deep insight. You're never content with superficialities. And since you feel the wisdom you hope to find is in books or within yourself, rather than in the hustle and bustle of daily living, you seek the peace and quiet in which to meditate. Studious, theoretical, and introspective, you seek to be an authority in some particular branch of knowledge or in some profession, gaining such in-depth expertise that perhaps only other experts in your field can understand you. It's not that you strive to shut others out; it's just that you yourself get so deeply involved in your subject that you don't realize you're leaving the average person behind.

You like to analyze, examine, and dissect anything and everything down to the minutest detail, trying to get to the heart of things and understand how they operate. But this activity usually takes place on the mental plane; you're not a hands-on person who can repair anything from a car engine to a malfunctioning toaster, or even an expert in specialized fields such as electronics. All of these are more or less practical areas as far as you're concerned, and you may be less adept in them than the average person. What interests you, what truly piques your curiosity, is trying to penetrate philosophical, metaphysical, and spiritual laws to find true values and underlying meanings.

There is a distinctly occult and mystical side to the number 7, and accordingly, you may have considerable intuition. If so, you will cherish the penetrating insights your intuition gives you. The only trouble with all this mental activity is that it may make you withdraw from the practical realities of life to live in your own ivory tower, untouched by everyday problems and ordinary human needs. But that doesn't bother you, because you dislike the noise and confusion of the business world; you hate manual labor, routine, and details. It's not your ambition to come to grips with the realities of life, to face aggressive competition or cope pragmatically with problems. Far from it.

You're also somewhat lacking in material ambition. Unless something else in your numerology chart indicates a desire for money, you would be more content in your quiet corner on a moderate income than battling the world to get your share of its wealth. You love the country, especially the plants and animals found there, and are especially fond of being near water Ideally, you would like to have a house in the country, away from the hustle and bustle and crowds of cities. Yet oddly enough, you fear extreme loneliness and poverty; you're not able to truly relax in your ivory tower because you feel you may someday need the friendships and worldly goods you have been brushing aside.

At some point in your life you may want to get married. And despite your high and somewhat isolating personal aims, you may actually do so. But the marriage may not be a happy one. For you tend to be shy and rather withdrawn, and with your philosophical otherworldly bent, you may lack the capacity to make the realistic adjustments that are necessary when two people live together. Furthermore, though your feelings are deep, you have a horror of showing them, lest someone else see into the most secret, intimate part of yourself. So your marriage partner might find you too reserved and aloof, or lacking in sympathy and understanding. Also, since you do not always communicate well, and are not skillful at the banalities and trivialities of casual conversation, it would be almost impossible for you to engage in pillow talk with the one you love. These "sweet nothings" would seem to you incredibly silly and meaningless! Besides, you feel it drains your energies to have too much contact with people; you would much rather spend your time quietly by yourself, to recharge your strength for your pursuits. Understandably, this is the kind of attitude that a romantic partner might find hard to live with.

But don't despair, there are still compatible mates for you! Individualistic 1 and 5 are good possibilities, since they're both independent enough not to mind when you withdraw into your shell. Cause-oriented 9, always busy with its own concerns, might also prove compatible—especially if you share an interest in the same cause—and like 1 and 5, 9 won't be emotionally dependent on you. But childlike 3 would undoubtedly find you too solemn and too deep for its superficial taste.

With the even numbers—2, 4, 6, and 8—you have virtually nothing in common. The adjustments and compromises that come so easily to 2 and 6, enabling them to get along with most people, are impossible for you. Of course they might be willing to put up with your need to be alone at times, since they'd do almost anything to preserve the peace; but what they absolutely can't stand is your emotional coolness and your refusal to let them really share your thoughts and feelings. The materialism of 4 and 8 mixes uncomfortably with your spiritual inclinations; you're convinced their viewpoint is totally wrong, and they think the same of you. Being a perfectionist yourself, you might feel some sympathy with the slow, cautious, conscientious ways of 4, but that isn't enough to bridge the gap between you.

All of the foregoing is written as if there were such a thing as a "number 7 person." But actually, there isn't. Besides the various numbers in each name, there are five special numbers: Soul Urge, Latent, Expression, Life Path, and Life Purpose numbers. (Refer to Chapter II if you need to refresh your memory on what each of these numbers means and how they are derived.) Thus, the preceding description is actually of the number 7 itself, not of any specific type of person, and the qualities delineated apply wherever a 7 appears in your numerology chart. However, if this number holds one of the special positions in your chart, there are slight variations on the 7 qualities, as follows:

If 7 is your Soul Urge: A perfectionist, a specialist, and a deep thinker, you reject the merely superficial and always seek to get to the heart of whatever you are studying. Your deepest desire is to grow both spiritually and in wisdom, and the success and material rewards on which other people set so much store are unimportant to you. Striving to develop your inner resources, you begin to understand the true meaning of life. In order to achieve your intellectual and immaterial goals, you feel you need peace and quiet, preferably in the country, where you do not need to contend with the hustle and bustle of daily life or interact with many people. Anything sudden, new, or short-lived distracts you; instead you seek to surround yourself with possessions of lasting value, whose richness increases and mellows with time. In your quiet corner of the world you will derive pleasure from being consulted by people who seek the benefit of your wisdom. Otherwise, though, you have no desire for socializing or easy popularity, and your aloofness makes it unlikely that you will ever have many friends. Yet you need to find strength within yourself to live your life happily in your own unique way. Otherwise you may begin to feel a sense of iolation, and wonder if you really *are* somebody different and special, or nothing more than a lonely misfit.

If 7 is your Latent number: You see yourself in a quiet, scholarly atmosphere, perhaps the library of your home. Though you have no great concern for money, there is much evidence of culture and refinement around you: rare books, beautiful pictures, carefully polished old furniture. Not surprisingly, what is new in style has no appeal to you. For you have always preferred to study the wisdom of the ancients rather than keep up with the latest headlines of each passing day.

If 7 is your Expression number: More refined, perhaps more spiritual than other people, you are a perfectionist and a specialist who has in some ways withdrawn from the world in order to develop in wisdom and inner strength. You tend to be solitary and self-sufficient, preferring your own company and your own deep thoughts to the superficial interests of most people around you. Since you are more concerned with inner truths than with practical realities or such rewards as fame and money, you lack any sort of material ambition. Nevertheless, you may succeed in spite of yourself because of your wisdom, for it's more than likely that people will seek out your advice in the area of your specialized knowledge.

If 7 is your Life Path number: You were meant to be a specialist and perfectionist, scientist and analyst, thinker and sage. You will have many opportunities to further your education, to study, meditate, and seek spiritual goals. For some reason you are different from most people, and you may often feel a sense of isolation from them. But it would be a mistake to try to be average, ordinary, adjusted to society, or aggressive in seeking material rewards. Your happiness comes from development of your inner resources, and rewards come to you when you do not chase them. If your Soul Urge or Expression number is 7, or if there is at least one 7 letter in your name (G, P, or Y), you will find it quite natural to follow your own path without regretting the everyday world you leave behind. But if you lack an added 7 influence, you may have to learn to concentrate and specialize, to cultivate your inner life. In any case, you should avoid seeking only superficial values and material rewards, because success in these areas will probably evade you.

If 7 is your Life Purpose number: This number represents the sum total of your personality and your life experiences. With 7 in this position, you can seek and find basic truths that eventually can add greatly to the whole world's store of wisdom.

CHAPTER XI

NUMBER 8

A POWERFUL, IMPORTANT PERSON WHO handles important matters capably and effectively—and who is well paid for doing so. Such is the vision of a number 8. Rather than pursue such subjective goals as inner peace or spiritual enlightenment, you seek success in the physical, material world. To have a business of your own, or at least to be a high executive in a major company, is the sort of position you strive for. You would also be happy as a money manager, financial adviser, stock broker, or in any other capacity connected with the making or handling of wealth.

You are not afraid to work hard to achieve success, but you prefer to deal only with large, important matters, leaving the details to others. In many ways you are like the number 4—who is also quite materialistic—but you are less concerned than 4 with the nitty-gritty of building for success. You think in more grand terms and are therefore often able to achieve greater heights than others imagine possible. You can easily view yourself as the company president who plans an operation, but you're far less impressed by the construction manager who actually gets the president's operation started. Broadness of vision is one of the things you strive for, and this can place you among the movers and shakers of the world, where your influence can be far-reaching.

Naturally, with your ambitious, expansive attitude, you are not inclined to be a shrinking violet. Recognition is important to you, and if others seem not to notice your successes you will not hesitate to point them out. This is not empty boasting but rather is born of a sincere belief that outstanding material achievement is a positive value, to be admired in the same way people admire someone who displays exceptional courage. Actually, you are one who realizes that achieving major success does require courage and the willingness to take risks—plus a host of other qualities, such as self-confidence, persistence, efficiency, decisiveness, and good judgment. You are proud that you possess these qualities, and you see no reason to hide that pride.

Yet you do not attempt to dominate or exercise any special influence over those on a lower corporate or material level than you. Instead, you are drawn to people whose success equals or outstrips your own, to those who have the power and money you either already have or are striving for. A struggle that matches you in business competition with another super-achiever is the kind that really excites and challenges you. And you like to socialize with such people because you feel they are living in the most effective way possible and in keeping with your own scale of values. It doesn't bother you to see them spend extravagantly on such amenities as penthouse apartments, expensive cars, yachts, or private jets, because you buy these things too, to the extent that your finances permit. It would do no good to point out that some of your money might more reasonably be used to help those in greater need than yourself. For you often find it hard to understand that not everyone is as well-endowed for achievement as you are. Even if you yourself rose from poor beginnings, or if you know other people who did, inwardly you probably feel that anyone could do the same if he or she tried hard enough.

If a subordinate shows some of the ambition and drive that are so vital to you, you will not hesitate to give that person a boost. You admire such upward striving and have enough confidence not to feel threatened by another's professional advances. You try to be objective in dealing with people, your balanced sense of values telling you it is not fair or efficient to do otherwise. Thus, you help those who show promise of being an asset to your company and try not to be unkind or unreasonably demanding toward other workers.

While this unemotional approach toward people may work well in business, it is often much less effective in personal relationships. After all, love can't be measured on a balance sheet, although you may have a hard time coming to grips with that fact. And because of your objective attitude, your romantic partner and your family often suffers. You may feel you love them and are proud of them, and you are certainly giving them everything material they could desire. But it's difficult for you to devote your time to their personal and emotional affairs, because it is business relationships, rather than personal liaisons, that really interest you.

To choose a compatible mate you would probably seek someone who possesses the same qualities you look for in business: someone who's helpful and accommodating, willing to make whatever adjustments are necessary to assure your joint success—or someone who could actively work along with you toward that success. This would suggest a 2 or a 6, who would gladly subordinate their needs to yours and take on your burdens. Practical, logical 4 would be well-suited to your sensibilities as well, as would be another 8—though two compulsively achieving 8s in one household might be too much of a good thing. The emotional side of these relationships would be sorely lacking, although that wouldn't bother you.

With the odd numbers—1, 3, 5, 7, and 9—you have no basic compatibility, though each of these individualists might be successful enough in his or her own way to win your respect. But all of these numbers are alike in that they have different motives than simply money-making to lead them on; and you would not understand this any more than they would understand your wholly materialistic values.

* * *

All of the foregoing is written as if there were such a thing as a "number 8 person." But actually, there isn't. Besides the various numbers in each name, there are five special numbers: Soul Urge, Latent, Expression, Life Path, and Life Purpose numbers. (Refer to Chapter II if you need to refresh your memory on what each of these numbers means and how they are derived.) Thus, the preceding description is actually of the number 8 itself, not of any specific type of person, and the qualities delineated apply wherever an 8 appears in your numerology chart. However, if this number holds one of the special positions in your chart, there are slight variations on the 8 qualities, as follows:

If 8 is your Soul Urge: Your orientation is toward big business, no matter who you are or what you do. The expansive operations of the commercial world excite you, and so does the thought of organizing and building something of your own—from a small business to an empire. There are natural leadership qualities in the number 8, and you want an opportunity to use them. You meet competition with enthusiasm and self-confidence, and you are happiest when there are challenges to test your strength. Your tendency is to think in rather grandiose terms, and you want everything around you to be on a large scale. This can make you a bit of a show-off, but on the positive side, it also makes you scorn pettiness or double-dealing. You strive to win fairly and honestly, on the strength of the powerful, idealistic personality you pride yourself in possessing. But these admirable qualities can sometimes be exaggerated in an unconstructive manner. From time to time you need to remind yourself that not everyone is geared to keep up with your rapid pace—and that some would *choose* not to even if they could. In striving to get ahead, you need to stop occasionally to help others; you should broaden your vision enough to realize that values other than your own may be equally valid.

If 8 is your Latent number: You see yourself as a VIP—influential, successful, and wealthy. Everything you do is on a large scale. For instance, you are far more likely to be the head of a multinational firm dealing in diversified products than the manager of a small local grocery store. You think of yourself as the kind of person who gets elected to the board of directors of major companies or societies, who is consulted by statesmen for your views on economic issues. The atmosphere around you is that of a richly furnished suite of offices where you preside decisively over many subordinates.

If 8 is your Expression number: You are naturally oriented toward big business and material success. You exercise good judgment and possess an innate ability to supervise people and to handle money. Financial rewards tend to come easily to you, because you know exactly what you want and are not held back by indecision or self-doubt. Highly ambitious, your goals are not vague or personal; you know without any reservations that above all you seek money, power, and recognition. The business of business excites you passionately, and as long as you are doing something that challenges your talents—and are being well reimbursed for your efforts—you never count the hours spent on the job. Yours is an attractive personality—broad and accepting in viewpoint, generous, fair-minded, and cheerful. As a supervisor, you can be very effective because of your leadership qualities, though in your personal life you may be lacking somewhat in sentiment or sensitivity.

If 8 is your Life Path number: You were meant to be an achiever in the material world, a practical, efficient, well-balanced organizer and manager of large enterprises. You will have many opportunities to attain wealth and power, and to exercise authority either in your own business or as a high-level executive in a large corporation. Good judgment concerning the management of money is the most important quality for you to cultivate, since too much concentration on either getting it or spending it can distort your perspective. If your Soul Urge or Expression number is 8, or if there is at least one 8 letter in your name (H, Q, or Z), you will have no problem achieving a grand material success. Lacking either of these, it is very important for you to cultivate balance, efficiency, and good judgment in all affairs—but most especially in financial management. Poor judgment in this area may lead to failure despite your many other good qualities and your hard work.

If 8 is your Life Purpose number: This number represents the sum total of your personality and your life experiences. With 8 in this position, you were not meant simply to make money for yourself, but to contribute to the development of the world's material resources for the benefit of all.

CHAPTER XII

NUMBER 9

BIG BROTHER OR SISTER TO ALL THE world, humanitarian and philanthropist—this is the nature of universally loving, giving 9. You try to see the good qualities in everyone and to focus on the likenesses between human beings rather than the differences. The idea of unselfish service to mankind, without thought of personal gain or reward, is very appealing to you. And if your circumstances permit, you might very well volunteer your services in some war-torn or poverty-stricken corner of the world to help care for the wounded and feed the hungry. Not only do you desire to be a healer and a dispenser of material aid and know-how, you want to be creative and artistic as well, to share your enjoyment of the beauty in the world with others.

It's a tall order, however, and you may exhaust yourself trying to be everything to everyone and making too many promises you can't possibly keep. Yet you have little time to spare for worrying about your own comfort. Even if you wear yourself out with your generosity, you'll probably feel the self-sacrifice was worthwhile. Short of giving your life for humanity, you are ready to give all your time and effort to any cause that seems to you to be for the benefit of others. In fact, the broader the scope of the cause, the more it appeals to you.

Universality is one of the things you strive for. You think in terms of helping the entire world rather than just your own small corner. Political causes may be especially attractive to you since they affect a wide range of people. Whether they're labeled liberal or conservative is beside the point; what matters is that you believe that the issues or platforms you are advocating are for the general good.

Wise and intuitive, with a broad, idealistic vision and enthusiasm for life and its possibilities, you are a most attractive personality who can be an inspiration to many. Your compassion and sympathy for other human beings is boundless, and you always seem to have a few minutes to spare to listen to other people's troubles. Yet your overflowing emotions can sometimes be counterproductive. You tend to commit yourself to too many things, spreading yourself so thin that you don't have the time or the strength to follow through on all of your projects. Or, you may simply forget what you were supposed to do because you're so busy trying to go in all directions at once. Control of your emotions and maintaining some sort of order in your life is necessary in order to keep it from becoming too complicated and overwhelming.

While you are generous with your time and energy, you also tend to give money freely. You may spend your own—as well as everyone else's—in the course of trying to help other people. Therefore, for all your good intentions, your efforts risk becoming somewhat ineffectual unless you can learn to apply some common sense and practicality. Learning to exert some self-restraint can be a boon to your effectiveness. Of course, you might also be able to get practical assistance from others, for your selfless giving sometimes draws help from unexpected quarters.

In romance, your overflowing emotional warmth can be lovable and yet create problems. You tend to fall in love easily and indiscriminately, but you are inclined to be more in love with the *idea* of love than with any particular individual. It is hard for one with your leanings toward universality to concentrate on one person. The most romantic of all the numbers, you always respond warmly to people. But this places you on the horns of a dilemma: You want to love individuals, and you want to love all of mankind, so your emotional life tends to become overcomplicated. You can't imagine taking an impersonal attitude in your relationships, but it's equally impossible for you to accept being tied down or possessed. As a result, you usually wind up suffering through your emotional experiences—but this doesn't stop you from trying again and again to find a lasting romantic relationship! The idea of being in love is too appealing for you to cut it out of your life, regardless of how much you may suffer.

Naturally, there are some numbers with whom you have a better chance for happiness than others.

Still, as in all other areas of your life, you're divided here too: You like the gentleness and emotional warmth of 2 and 6, but you find their self-protective way of life limiting. On the other hand, you like emotionally independent 1, 3, and 5, but consider them rather unresponsive to your easily aroused feelings. Though you have little in common with withdrawn 7, romantically speaking, you may have some rapport with this number on a spiritual or intuitive level. With 4 and 8, however, the potential problems are overwhelming; their materialism will strain even your boundless capacity for love, since material matters are so alien to your way of thinking.

All of the foregoing is written as if there were such a thing as a "number 9 person." But actually, there isn't. Besides the various numbers in each name, there are five special numbers: Soul Urge, Latent, Expression, Life Path, and Life Purpose numbers. (Refer to Chapter II if you need to refresh your memory of what each of these numbers means and how they are derived.) Thus, the preceding description is actually of the number 9 itself, not of any specific type of person, and the qualities delineated apply wherever a 9 appears in your numerology chart. However, if this number holds one of the special positions in your chart, there are slight variations on the 9 qualities, as follows:

If 9 is your Soul Urge: You want to love and help everyone, and to be loved by all in return. Highly emotional and warmly sympathetic, you are a joiner of all sorts of groups involved with worthy causes, and you may often be seen at demonstrations calling attention to the issues you want to promote. You strive to be self-forgetful in your concern for others, and you are willing to subject yourself to discomfort, difficulty, and even danger for the cause of humanity. Not ambitious for material gain or personal rewards, you yearn to invest all your time, talent, and money so that all humanity may benefit. But there is a danger in your overexpansiveness: You may want to give more than other people are able to receive, with the result that you'll simply be meddling in their lives rather than achieving the beneficial effects you intended. Or you may give too much and then become bitter because of others' lack of appreciation. In trying to help in such a wide variety of ways, you may spread yourself too thin, exhausting yourself and not completing any of the projects you started.

If 9 is your Latent number: You see yourself as best friend to the entire world, overflowing with a love for humanity and an eagerness to be of service. You have a magnetic personality and are generous, friendly, and well-liked. You understand and sympathize with other people's feelings and can always be appealed to for help and advice. It pleases you to think of yourself as having risen above your own struggles and problems so as to be able to dedicate yourself to helping others overcome theirs.

If 9 is your Expression number: A humanitarian, serving the world with love, compassion, and understanding, is the personality you express. You are totally lacking in material ambition. Altruistic and broad-minded, you are capable of universal tolerance, fellowship, and goodwill. Loving all of mankind, you are naturally cause-oriented and get very excited about the problems of entire nations or of people with whom you have no direct connection. Because of this you are attracted to broad areas of service such as politics, reform movements, social work, and teaching. You long for love and personal happiness, but they tend to elude you; since your greatest pleasure is achieved by transcending your own experiences and helping others, there's not much time or energy to spare for personal relationships. For you, to give is indeed a gift to yourself, as long as you restrain yourself enough to offer only what others are capable of receiving.

If 9 is your Life Path number: You were meant to be a humanitarian and a passionate advocate of any cause that will benefit mankind generally. You will have many opportunities to offer help, sympathy, and inspiration to others—not only in your personal circle of contacts but in some broader area. You need to cultivate tolerance toward all kinds and classes of people, realizing that everyone is a part of the universal totality of the human race, or, as it is more commonly expressed, that all men are brothers. If your Soul Urge or Expression number is 9, or if there is at least one 9 letter in your name (I or R), you will encounter few obstacles in your humanitarian quests. Lacking an added 9 influence, however, you must consciously strive for a broader vision and a generosity of spirit. It will be worth the extra effort, for only when you act toward others with tolerance, compassion, and understanding can you find happiness for yourself.

If 9 is your Life Purpose number: This number represents the sum total of your personality and your life experiences. With 9 in this position, you receive the greatest benefit by giving. And as your concern with helping others grows, so will the sphere of your influence widen.

CHAPTER XIII

the master numbers: 11 and 22

BY NOW YOU ARE AWARE THAT NUMERology uses only the numbers from 1 through 9, and that all numbers of over two digits are reduced to one. There are two exceptions to this, however—the so-called "master numbers," 11 and 22. These are said to be the "higher octave" of 2 (1 + 1) and 4 (2 + 2), respectively. Thus 11 has a lot of qualities of 2, and 22 embodies many of the 4 characteristics. But the master numbers also have special, more expansive characteristics. It is important to note that the somewhat mystical qualities associated with these numbers do not have any great effect on a person's everyday life—on the business or personal or even romantic consideration that concern us day to day. So for most of us they rarely come into play in any sort of practical, hands-on manner. Rather, they embody many of the characteristics of 2 and 4, but place them on an unusually high plane, as you'll see below.

Incidentally, 11 and 22 are never used in the

numbers that represent the letters in your name; 1 through 9 are the numbers used for that. Only when adding up the vowels or consonants in your name to find your Soul Urge, Latent, and Expression numbers, when adding up your birth date to find you Life Path number, or when adding up your name and your birth date to find your Life Purpose number, do 11 and 22 occasionally arise. Because of this, 11 and 22 are not as important for numerological analysis as the numbers 1 through 9. But whenever you do encounter 11 or 22 you might want to remember that they are similar to 2 and 4, respectively, with the following special characteristics:

NUMBER 11

You want to live on a higher plane than the rest of humanity—not in an egotistical way but as an inspirational leader. You may have great intuition and psychic ability, or a special interest in religious or spiritual matters, which you will want to share with the world. Unlike 2 (1 + 1), which is rather shy and self-effacing, you long to be in the limelight; you are eager to attract attention and publicity so you can spread your ideas and have an influence, however small, on the lives of as many people as you can possibly reach. Whereas 2 tends to be very tactful and cooperative in a personal way, you strive to bring peace, harmony, and high ideals to the world in a far-reaching, general manner which can benefit more than just those people in your immediate circle. This is a positive goal which adds to your charisma and your image as an idealistic, inspirational leader.

A passion for salvation and an uplifted psyche motivates your efforts. But unlike 2, which has almost too much sympathy for and understanding of individual problems, you try to lead people in the direction you feel they should go, regardless of their individual needs and desires. No one could deny that your intentions are good. It's just that you can't help but think in universal rather than personal terms. Although you know what is good for the world you may not be able to help a specific person with a specific problem. Yet even though you may be more successful as a propagandist than you are in dealing with specific personal issues, you attract others by the sheer force of your personality and the beauty of your ideals.

NUMBER 22

Since 22 is the highest number used in numerology, if it is found in your chart it is an indication that your goals are very lofty indeed. While the number 4 (2 + 2) is concerned with physical form and constructive building on a material level, the motivation of 22 is to go even further—to build perfectly and permanently for the benefit and security of all. Your desire is no less than to master material things, including money, so that whatever you do turns out right and is practical, profitable, and worthwhile. It is said of 22 that its eyes are on the stars while its feet are firmly on the ground. This attitude comes naturally to you, and you strive to achieve a combination of idealism and practicality. You realize the necessity for being realistic in a basically materialistic world, yet you would not want to make something useless or shoddy just to reap a quick profit. Wealth as an end in itself does not appeal to you, since you see money as simply a by-product of your prime concern, the ability to deal with life on the materialistic plane and come out a winner.

You possess the dependability, loyalty, honesty, and the methodical, well-organized work habits of the number 4. But your ideals are much higher, your viewpoint much broader, than 4's. While 4 is content to work along rather routine lines and to strive for accomplishments within his or her immediate environment, you think in terms of planning the economy of a country or even the world. Without forgetting the realities of a situation you try to see its broader implications. You have a talent for being both practical and theoretical, for seeing situations as they are without blinding yourself to other possibilities. This is a rare gift, since many people either get bogged down in technical details or have lots of ideas but no real knowledge of how to put them into practice.

With all these talents you cannot help but accomplish worthwhile goals. Your only problem is that you may not always aim high enough; thus you risk dropping down to the routine level of 4, content with a lesser (although quite reasonable!) amount of success within a relatively small scope.

CHAPTER XIV

ARE YOU MISSING ANY NUMBERS?

UNTIL NOW WE HAVE BEEN CONSIDERING what the numbers mean and what they indicate when they appear in various places in your numerology chart. But, regardless of how long your name is, chances are there will be one or more letters missing. More precisely, there may be no A, S, or J (number 1); B, K, or T (2); C, L, or U (3); D, M, or V (4); E, N, or W (5); F, O, or X (6); G, P, or Y (7); H, Q, or Z (8); or I and R (9).

To numerologists, many of whom believe in reincarnation, these missing numbers are said to represent lessons you failed to learn in a past life and which will now cause you difficulty until they are learned. According to this theory, if a number which is missing from your name or birth date appears elsewhere in your chart—as your Soul Urge, or Latent, Expression, or Life Path number—you are working at overcoming the lack in yourself. Life will bring you many opportunities to do so, although it will not be as easy for you to handle such situations as it is for someone who does not suffer from the same numerical lack in their name or birth date.

Whether or not you choose to believe this explanation, the fact remains that the effect of missing numbers in a person's chart is often quite visible in their character or life experiences. This may be easier to see in other people than in ourselves, for it's a rare individual who can view his or her faults realistically. But whether or not you are able to pinpoint missing numerological elements in yourself or someone else, they may be a powerful factor in your personality and experiences—or in those of your lover. For generally, they signal inner conflicts, difficulties in dealing with a particular area of life, an inability to handle material matters, or any number of other potential stumbling blocks. And, of course, anything that causes trouble for one partner in a relationship is going to affect the relationship itself, either directly or indirectly.

In the preceding chapters you learned the meanings of the numbers. Now we will discuss specifically the impact on an individual's personalty and life when they *lack* certain numbers. (Incidentally, a person whose chart lacks a number is known as a "Minus-1," a "Minus-2," or whatever the case may be.) If you find that your own name or that of your romantic interest has one or more numbers lacking, do not be dismayed. Just about everyone does! It is helpful to look at these missing numbers not as faults but as opportunities and challenges to improve in the areas indicated by the lack(s). Your minuses may prove to be quite in keeping with the chart of someone you care about and vice versa! They are merely another indication of ways in which you may or may not get along with someone else. In fact, a person in whose chart there are no lacks is often a nonachiever; he is popular, and good things come easily, so he simply is never stimulated to make any particular effort.

The chart of an individual that shows only one lack indicates a person who has at least one direction in which to strive. However, this may sometimes lead him to overcompensate and become obsessive in that direction. It's important to remember that the ideal is balance, not overemphasis in any particular direction. So if you or your lover are minus only one number, be aware of this and try to control the tendency to concentrate too much energy in one place. It could be either a minor or a major problem to the individual or a relationship, depending on whether the concentration is a mild quirk or an unreasonable, perhaps self-destructive, obsession.

In charts that are minus two or more numbers there is of course less of a desire to devote yourself to one particular area of improvement. Problems in a variety of different areas may be indicated. This does not necessarily mean a person with such a numerology chart is hard to get along with, or is a hopeless nonachiever. He may very well be tackling his problems in a positive way and developing himself in many directions.

Then again, a Minus-2 (or more) person might yield to negativity, claiming he can't cope with all his difficulties and refusing even to try. Which way it will go is partly dependent on which particular numbers are missing, partly on the rest of the chart, and partly on timing. If he is in a cycle whose Pinnacle number counteracts the influence of one of his lacking numbers, he will find it easier to compensate for any negative influence. Especially in the case where his Pinnacle number is the same as his Soul Urge or Expression, for instance, he'll probably find that things that are usually difficult are made just a little bit easier and will be encouraged to take a positive attitude.

If in appraising the chart of that special someone—the man or woman of your dreams—you find several minuses, this is by no means a reason for dropping your mate. Some missing numbers have a more directly damaging effect on relationships than others, as you will find from the descriptions on the following pages. The compatibility between your chart and your mate's is also very important: Looking into the numbers, you may be able to help your loved one face problems with a positive attitude. Your sympathy and understanding may be just what's needed to overcome and avoid problems posed by missing numbers. By comparing your entire charts, you'll be able to understand which elements are affecting you. This in turn will give you the free will to face life courageously rather than let it defeat you.

Now let's move on to a consideration of the individual lacks in the name chart:

Minus-1 (lack of any As, Js, or Ss): This shows a lack of individuality and an unwillingness to push yourself forward in the world. You don't want to take the initiative or to move ahead of the pack, for fear of finding yourself out on a limb all alone. Lacking self-confidence, you will shrink from situations where you have to sell yourself or your ideas or talents. Fearing to be wrong, you avoid making decisions or facing issues squarely. Although you may have an innate leadership ability, you find it easier and safer to be a follower, making yourself inconspicuous within a group. The Minus-1 person tends to be less of an achiever than his talents would indicate, unless he grits his teeth and forces himself to push forward even when he would rather hang back. In a relationship, Minus-1 is generally attracted to understanding partners. Those who lavish praise and encouragement on Minus-1 can be a big factor in his or her success. A more aggressive partner, however, may totally overwhelm this number, with the result that Minus-1 could lose what confidence and individuality he or she *does* have.

Minus-2 (lack of Bs, Ks, or Ts): The inability to blend your individuality with that of others is the main obstacle confronting a Minus-2. As one might imagine, this can prove to be quite important when it comes to love, since a sensitive partner will often be hurt by the lack of thoughtfulness this attitude often bears with it. With a Minus-2, you are busy projecting yourself and forwarding your own needs, interests, and desires. If you do something nice for your partner—buy flowers or some other gift, for instance—it's because *you* want to do it, not because of any special sensitivity to your mate's unspoken desires and messages about what *he* or *she* would like you to do. On a more general level, a Minus-2 often means that you lack the patience and ability to deal with details that are among the talents of 2. This can be a problem at work and in other areas of your life, when little things you didn't bother to attend to become increasingly big problems. Also, lacking 2's ability to accumulate, you may be careless with your money and possessions, letting them get lost or slip through your fingers. Of course, a partner with the right, thoughtful influence might very well be able to help you overcome some of these problems by pointing out the details you neglect or—better yet—by picking up after you.

Minus-3 (lack of any Cs, Ls, or Us): In many ways you are extremely serious, not exactly a lighthearted, fun person. Considering the sense of humor of 3, the playfulness and childlike delight this number takes in entertaining others and being noticed and admired, a lack of 3 indicates that you'll have to work extra hard to develop or appreciate these qualities. You have very little sense of humor. Stories and jokes that bring roars of laughter from all your friends hardly provoke a smile from you. It's not that you have any objection to being amused; it's simply that you find very few things genuinely amusing. When it comes to parties, too, you tend to look on in wonder at the antics and carrying on, finding it all silly and tiresome. You shudder at the thought that you might be expected to do a little performing yourself, and in fact you hate to draw attention to yourself in any setting. Like Minus-1, you always try to stay in the background. The need for a certain anonymity is so strong that you often slump or are round-shouldered from your continued efforts to draw yourself as much as possible into a self-protective ball. While this does not detract from other wonderful qualities you possess, your mate might complain that you are sometimes unable to open up fully and communicate, even with them! Otherwise, Minus-3 need not pose any important romantic problems, especially if you choose a partner who shares your serious outlook on life, not a party animal.

Minus-4 (lack of Ds, Ms, or Vs): Working hard has little appeal for the Minus-4. For you, there's no thrill in planning a project or building slowly toward a successful goal; you simply cannot understand the pleasure some people get from the building, nor do you take pride in the skills and the feeling involved in constructing something of value. You resent the need for self-discipline in sticking to a job—any job—especially when it proves difficult, boring, or repetitious. You cannot help but feel such work is intruding on time you'd rather use doing other things. Shortcuts and quick-fix solutions are your style, and whenever possible you'll delegate work to others or use that age-old excuse, "That's not my job." Although you may seem to be working hard all the time—and have perhaps convinced even yourself that you are—in actuality you often accomplish little. In romance, this Minus-4 tendency generally manifests itself in careless housekeeping, repairs that remain undone, constant complaints about job pressures, and lack of any budgeting or financial planning. You'll have to keep a constant lookout to keep these from getting out of control. And an understanding mate, one that enjoys taking care of others, will help keep your household—and your love—running smoothly.

Minus-5 (lack of Es, Ns, or Ws: Since E is the most commonly used letter in the alphabet, and N and W are also relatively common, it is rare to find a name that is Minus-5. However, when it does happen, the person is usually marked by a certain lack of ability to be touched by life experiences. If you are a Minus-5, you may be afraid of change, since your adaptability and versatility will be more limited than that of people with this number. Often, you'll find it difficult to adjust to new circumstances, convinced that change can only be for the worse. You are the type who will resist changing homes, for instance. And if ever you are forced to move anyway, you'll never quite feel at home in your new place. This is your attitude toward all of life, in fact. But remember, you can often be your own worst enemy by fighting to hold back change instead of looking for new opportunities in the future. Even in love, when you settle into a relationship, you're in for the duration! Any change may seem threatening to you. Certainly you will have no interest in a potential partner who is quite different from you, for this would necessarily involve the transformation and compromise you dislike. So, try to find a partner who shares your views, because there's no room for change or compromise here, and differences in feeling and opinion could lead to a major blowout.

Minus-6 (lack of any Fs, Os, or Xs): Since 6 is the basic partnership number, a Minus-6 is necessarily a big drawback to long-lasting love. It's not that you avoid romance, or even marriage. Instead, you tend to jump from one relationship to another, convinced at each step that this time it's true love. And, sometimes, it may actually *be* love: Minus-6 doesn't impair your ability to love, just your ability to make the adjustments necessary to *keep* love alive for long periods of time. Not wanting to be tied down or to take on any responsibility, you may enjoy living with a partner but will back off from the thought of marriage and children, buying a home, and so forth. Although in theory these things are thought to be joyful, since they are done in conjunction with someone you love, to you responsibilities are simply a drag and take all the fun out of relationships. And just as you dislike facing responsibilities in love, you also try to avoid other obligations—toward your family, job, community, or anything else. If, for instance, circumstances force you to take on the care of an aging relative or a handicapped child, you may be very resentful.

Minus-7 (lack of any Gs, Ps, or Ys): Inner resources, including a sustaining spiritual belief, are related to 7, so the lack of this number indicates a dislike of being alone. Yet you may not really fit well in groups, either sometimes feeling lonely in a crowd. You tend to be "different," a little bit odd somehow. You're probably bookish and a scholar, yet, lacking 7's intellectual side; you may be lazier about getting down to fundamentals than some scholars. On the other hand, you may very well overcompensate for the missing 7 qualities, becoming very knowledgeable, perhaps in some odd, very personal area of interest. Minus-7 is unable to get much pleasure out of sex or other demonstrations of affection, which quite obviously could put a damper on romance! Since this lack hinders your ability to achieve a feeling of intimacy, both you and your partner need to invest extra effort in communicating with each other. In the end, however, Minus-7's inner sense of isolation may make a truly intimate relationship difficult.

Minus-8 (lack of any Hs, Qs, or Zs): Money management is the main talent associated with 8, and a lack of this number indicates carelessness or inefficiency in handling financial matters. If you forget to record checks you've paid out and are constantly finding that your bank account is overdrawn and your checkbook is impossible to balance, chances are you're a Minus-8. Your timing may be off; you may pass up good money-making opportunities and then take the plunge just when wiser investors are pulling out. Minus-8 doesn't necessarily mean you're *always* short of cash. You may, in fact, be excellent at making money or lucky at acquiring it, through inheritance, for instance. It's what you do with the money after you get it that's questionable! Perhaps you are a compulsive gambler at the casinos and racetracks or in the stock market; you pile up huge profits but don't have the good sense to quit while you're ahead, to take your winnings and go off and enjoy them. Such is the typical fate of a Minus-8. Thank goodness that in most relationships financial matters take a back seat to more emotional considerations. But still, when there's a vast difference between your attitude toward money and your partner's, this may cause the kind of conflict that even love can't cure. So it's vitally important for you to discuss money matters with your mate, and to compromise where possible. An understanding partner may be able to compensate for your poor money management.

Minus-9 (lack of any Is or Rs): Universality and humanitarianism are strongly connected with 9, so those who lack this number are generally the kind of people who "don't want to get involved." You are basically self-absorbed. If you are in reasonably comfortable circumstances, it's almost impossible for you to imagine what life might be like for people who are less fortunate. And this is as true of your friends, relatives, and neighbors as it is of people with whom you have no direct connection. The sweeping, all-men-are-brothers feeling connected with 9 will arouse in you no real sympathy, though you may occasionally contribute to what your philosophical or religious principles tell you is a worthy cause. If, on the other hand, you try to compensate for your missing 9, you may become involved in all sorts of exotic projects, from wildlife conservation in Africa to health care programs in India, to the preservation of native crafts in Ecuador. Still, while you may promote these or other causes with all the energy you possess, your involvement is more intellectual than emotional. You may quite possibly have no desire at all for hands-on contact with the beneficiaries of your help. Minus-9 may have little direct impact on your love life, since it is a universal vibration rather than a personal one. So you'll probably soar free to your romantic heights! However, you may find you have little patience for a partner who's a sucker for hard-luck stories, or for one who is constantly changing plans—or more likely your *joint* plans—in order to help others.

You can see that minuses in a name chart are a factor to be reckoned with in assessing compatibility—though not necessarily a deterrent to harmony between two people. The most important thing to remember about the minuses is that they are constantly forced on our attention in one way or another. For instance, everyone needs and is interested in money, but to the average person this is only one of many needs, along with love, friendship, security, and the like. To the Minus-8, though, money is always in the forefront of his mind, either because he has too much or too little. In the same way, a person with 6 in his chart, after a failed marriage, may have no particular enthusiasm for marrying again. But a Minus-6 may have a compulsion to make a success of marriage and keep trying it with different partners, hoping eventually to find that perfect relationship.

So, bearing in mind this emphasis on the minuses, try to trace their effect on your own or your partner's life. Then, try to determine whether these effects are the kind you can live with, overcome, or compensate for—or whether they are so potentially destructive they will bring only romantic disaster.

CHAPTER XV

Putting It All Together

IN THE PRECEDING CHAPTERS YOU HAVE discovered how to make a numerology chart and find your own numerical vibrations. You have also learned what each individual number means and the many ways it can impact on your life. But when assessing your own chart, a friend's, or the compatibility of two charts to each other, there is one more step to take. What numerologists call an "Inclusion Table" shows you at a glance what is termed the "weight" of a chart—the overall tendencies, as opposed to the meanings of the individual numbers of which the chart is composed.

The following pages give you some examples of Inclusion Charts and what they can reveal. Naturally, it would be impossible here to cover all conceivable variations; they would run into the thousands. But with these examples to point you in the right direction, you can start making your own assessments. (Incidentally, the names used here are not those of any specific people; any resemblance to real people is strictly coincidental.)

The Inclusion Table is made quite simply by listing numbers from 1 through 9 and noting beside them the letters in an individual's name that correspond to those numbers.

Example 1: MICHAEL JAMES COLLINS

1	A J A S S
2	—
3	C L C L L
4	M M
5	E E N
6	O
7	—
8	H
9	I I

First is should be noted that, since 5 is considered the most common number, to compensate for this in an Inclusion Table it's a good idea to mentally deduct one or two 5s before the total number of 5s is taken into account with respect to the table as a whole. Thus, in the example above there is, in effect, only one 5—not an extraordinary quantity and not out of line with the quantity of 4s, 6s, 8s, and 9s in this particular name.

Once that's done it becomes obvious where the real strength in Michael's personality lies—he is unusually well endowed with the originality, initiative, and leadership qualities of 1, and the creative, self-expressive, somewhat show-off qualities of 3. This is a man who is gifted with many ideas and many talents, and he isn't shy about promoting himself and bringing his talents to the attention of those who can help him get ahead. In fact, he enjoys the spotlight and is possibly even something of a publicity-seeker, promoting himself wherever he finds an audience willing to listen to him.

On the negative side, Michael lacks receptive, detail-minded 2 and scientific, perfectionist 7. He tends to go for "the big picture" and leave others to handle the routine of making his ideas operational. On a day-to-day level, he may lack basic knowledge about the area in which he works, and he may make no particular attempt to gain this knowledge. For instance, a salesman may be very successful in promoting a product even though he has only a superficial understanding of the methods and materials used in its manufacture. Fortunately for Michael, with his initiative, aggressiveness, and artistic talents he will probably wind up in a job where he has other people handling details for him and supplying the technical expertise he lacks. Being a Minus-2 and a Minus-7, Michael may secretly be a little in awe of those who are more practical and efficient than he is or who have better technical education than he does. Nevertheless, he probably likes himself well enough the way he is, and he's not about to quit his commanding position to go back to school and catch up on any technicalities he's missed.

As a romantic partner, Michael's Minus-2 and his abundance of self-promotion numbers suggest that he would be self-absorbed and self-propelling, finding it difficult to truly share his thoughts and plans with someone else or to be sensitive to his lover's desires and needs. However, many women will be attracted to his dynamic personality and may be willing to forgive his lack of sensitivity on the grounds that he's busy with important matters. A more difficult potential problem is posed by his Minus-7. This suggests a constant feeling of not quite belonging in whatever circumstances he finds himself, and accordingly Michael may have some difficulties with the physical side of love. (Remember that 7 is an intellectual and spiritual number, which somewhat withdraws from physical—in this case sexual—contact, and a lack of this number may have the effect of emphasizing this instinctive withdrawal.)

Example 2: KRISTIE DOWLING

1	S
2	K T
3	L
4	D
5	E W N
6	O
7	G
8	——
9	R I I I

Again, discounting one or two 5s, you can see that Kristie's numbers from 1 through 7 are evenly distributed, indicating that she has a reasonable share of the qualities associated with those numbers but no particular emphasis. Her focus is on humanitarian, universalist, and somewhat impractical 9.

And as if to further underline this impracticality, she is also lacking any of the vibrations of the money-management number, 8. So Kristie is a very sympathetic, concerned person, inclined to feel sorry for anyone in trouble, anywhere in the world, and very apt to become involved in promoting worthy causes. Yet money will always be a big factor in her life—probably not because of her own needs but in connection with her causes.

People who are actually of much help to others, as Kristie undoubtedly wants to be, have to be practical, good organizers and adept at managing finances—all the qualities Kristie lacks, because she's a Minus-8. Since a minus, as mentioned previously, keeps intruding into our lives, not only will she work for causes—which she likes to do and does well—she will also get involved in the financing of such projects. For instance, her sincerity and enthusiasm may help her win funding for a day-care center for welfare children; but then there's the problem of being able to juggle the various expenses over a period of time, and this Kristie will have trouble doing. In the end her project, for all the good intentions and high hopes with which it was started, may not be able to sustain itself. On a more personal level, she's probably the kind of person who feels rich when she first cashes her salary check, but within hours she manages to fritter away half the money, and by the end of the pay period she always winds up broke—no matter how large her earnings may be!

As a romantic partner, Kristie is a poor bet for a man who is highly ambitious and materialistic, or for a rigid and selfish man. A man who wants a lot of attention and ego stroking would resent the fact that she divides her love between him and the rest of the world. But many men would find her warm, caring attitude very appealing and would be more than willing to forgive her impracticality. By some, Kristie's inability to handle money might even be considered charmingly "feminine."

Example 3: ROBERT EDWYN GWEN

1	——
2	B T
3	——
4	D
5	E E W N W E N
6	O
7	Y G
8	——
9	R R

It is obvious that even after two 5s are deducted from the others in Robert's chart, 5 remains the most prominent number. This suggests that he is a rolling-stone type who loves the change, variety, and freedom of life. He can probably do many things well, and he's always interested in learning new skills. He's cooperative, gets along well with people, and tends to blend in wherever he goes. On the other hand, Robert is not a leader, as is indicated by his Minus-1. He lacks the creative bent of 3, and the money-managing qualities of 8. These minuses will probably become most prominent at work. For instance, if Robert is offered a management position requiring inventiveness and good financial management—which many jobs do—he will find such a position difficult. However, Robert's expansive, inquisitive nature may give him enough skills to compensate in one way or another for the qualities he lacks.

As a romantic partner, this cooperative, adaptable personality makes Robert easy to get along with. He may be an underachiever and a poor money manager, but a woman who is not too ambitious or demanding might prefer his pleasant companionship to the self-absorption of more goal-oriented types. But whereas Robert's need for variety and freedom is quite attractive and stimulating, a woman who was interested in him would need to be adaptable herself. If not, or if she fails to keep his interest, he might not be willing to make a romantic commitment. In a few years or months—or even weeks—Robert will probably be off looking for variety and adventure with a new companion.

These examples should not be taken as the exact definition of the charts used or any others that may be like them. Each number has many possibilities, and each person has a different background and life circumstances. But these examples will show you how to combine the broad general trends in a person's chart to show his or her overall possibilities, strengths, and weaknesses. The more you know about someone, the more plainly you can see how these general trends become specific factors in his or her life. Incidentally, this is something you should point out to your friends if you attempt to do their numerology charts. Some people like to challenge you by saying, "I'm not going to tell you anything; *you* tell *me*." This is poor policy, and you would be justified in refusing to do their chart at all if they won't cooperate.

There is one other important thing to remember when attempting to analyze Inclusion Tables: Life gives people many opportunities to overcome their numerological lacks, and often someone whose chart you work out is well on the way to doing just that. Thus, an individual with, for instance, a Minus-8 might be a financial officer of a corporation and doing very well. This indicates that he has rallied his personality assets to help him overcome his innate lack of money management skills. He is now working hard to wipe that minus off his chart, so to speak.

Numerological theory includes a belief in reincarnation, and claims that in each life we are required to work at overcoming what we did wrong in the last life, as symbolized by the minuses in our chart. That's why the opportunities to deal with the types of matters indicated by the minuses keep popping up in our lives, forcing us to try to cope with and overcome them. Whether or not you accept the theory of reincarnation, there's no question that the opportunities to grapple with your minuses do keep coming up. So don't assume that an individual is stuck with certain problems because of the minuses you see in his numerology chart. He might have compensated for his weaknesses at least to the point of being able to live with them painlessly. In fact, he might even have gotten to the point of overcompensating and turning an innate weakness into a real strength in his daily life.

So, with this in mind, you're ready to take stock of the numbers and use them to your greatest advantage. No longer will you be confused by your moods and desires, or by the quirks and complaints and charms of your mate. Rather than wait passively or anxiously for love to come to you, work actively with your numbers to find and keep a truly fulfilling relationship. Armed with an understanding of the power of numbers, you will indeed find that . . . It All Adds Up to Love!

ABOUT THE AUTHOR

Helen Tono has written over forty-eight books and thousands of articles about the occult, especially numerology and astrology. She lives in New York City.

In your quest for true love, let the heavens help you!
Bantam Books presents

the love life guides

A fun, sexy, and uninhibited series of forecasts, predictions, and compatibility guides for finding and keeping the perfect mate.

Starring Your Love Life: This comprehensive astrology guide includes compatibility match-ups and teasing strategies for attracting that perfect lover—no matter what their sign!

It All Adds Up to Love: Find romance by the numbers! The ancient science of numerology provides scintillating information and understanding of the most important numbers in life and love.

The Lover's Dream: Yes, dreams of love can come true! Learn to interpret and reprogram your dreams to solve your love dilemmas or find the perfect mate.

Tarot: Love is in the Cards: Unveil the mystery of the centuries-old Tarot, and discover how to stack the deck in your favour for love!

1 1 7 8 5 9 4

JOSEPH WARD

6 5 1

8 Latent

3 Soul Urge

Ex

1 5 1 5 9 4

JANIS WARD

1 9 1

7 Latent

1 SOUL URGE

MILLAR

9 1

SKELTON

5 6 2 3